UNDERSTANDING
JUDAISM

BY NEL YOMTOV

CONTENT CONSULTANT

David Nelson

Rabbi and Visiting Associate Professor of Religion
Bard College

Essential Library

An Imprint of Abdo Publishing | abdopublishing.com

UNDERSTANDING
WORLD RELIGIONS
AND BELIEFS

ABDOPUBLISHING.COM

Published by Abdo Publishing, a division of ABDO, PO Box 398166, Minneapolis, Minnesota 55439. Copyright © 2019 by Abdo Consulting Group, Inc. International copyrights reserved in all countries. No part of this book may be reproduced in any form without written permission from the publisher. Essential Library™ is a trademark and logo of Abdo Publishing.

Printed in the United States of America, North Mankato, Minnesota
032018
092018

THIS BOOK CONTAINS
RECYCLED MATERIALS

Cover Photo: Alexander D. Sabransky/Shutterstock Images
Interior Photos: Pascal Deloche/Godong/picture alliance/Godong/Newscom, 4–5, 54; Danny Drake/Press of Atlantic City/AP Images, 7; Red Line Editorial, 9, 45, 85; Anupam Nath/AP Images, 10; Fine Art Images/Heritage Images/Glow Images, 12–13; C. J. Macer/iStockphoto, 17; iStockphoto, 18; DEA Picture Library/De Agostini/Getty Images, 20–21; akg-images/British Library/Newscom, 26–27; Fine Art Images Heritage Images/Newscom, 30; Everett Historical/Shutterstock Images, 34; Shutterstock Images, 36–37, 46–47, 60 (left), 60 (right), 66–67, 70–71, 74–75; Renee Jones Schneider/TNS/Newscom, 40–41; Manuel Cohen Photography/Manuel Cohen/Newscom, 43; Rostislav Glinsky/Shutterstock Images, 48–49; Katherine Frey/The Washington Post/Getty Images, 56–57; Marcel Mettelsiefen/AP Images, 62; M. Spencer Green/AP Images, 64; Mike Cherim/iStockphoto, 72; Godong/Universal Images Group/Getty Images, 78–79; Ludek Perina/CTK/AP Images, 81; Murad Sezer/Reuters/Newscom, 82; Sean Locke Photography/Shutterstock Images, 89; Sebastian Scheiner/AP Images, 92–93; Bastiaan Slabbers/Sipa USA/AP Images, 98

Editor: Marie Pearson
Series Designer: Maggie Villaume

LIBRARY OF CONGRESS CONTROL NUMBER: 2017961412

PUBLISHER'S CATALOGING-IN-PUBLICATION DATA

Name: Yomtov, Nel, author.
Title: Understanding Judaism / by Nel Yomtov.
Description: Minneapolis, Minnesota : Abdo Publishing, 2019. | Series: Understanding world religions and beliefs | Includes online resources and index.
Identifiers: ISBN 9781532114274 (lib.bdg.) | ISBN 9781532154102 (ebook)
Subjects: LCSH: Judaism--Doctrines--Juvenile literature. | Judaism and culture--Juvenile literature. | World religions--Juvenile literature. | Religious belief--Juvenile literature.
Classification: DDC 296.0--dc23

CONTENTS

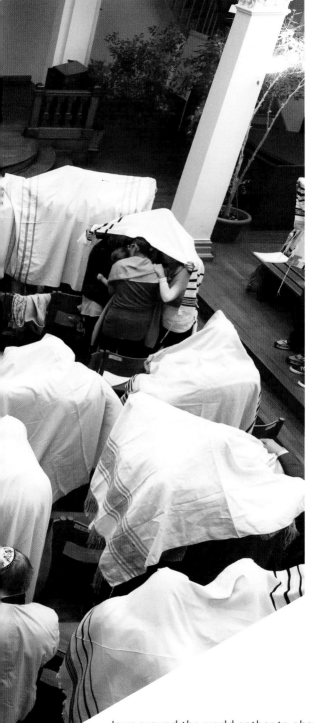

AN ANCIENT RELIGION

It is early evening, and the sun is beginning to set. Inside the synagogue, the Jewish house of worship, hundreds of people have gathered to observe the holiest of all holidays in the entire Jewish calendar—Yom Kippur. The holiday is known as the Day of Atonement, the day in which people of the Jewish faith ask God's forgiveness for the sins they have committed during the year. It is a solemn time when Jews acknowledge their shortcomings and vow to become better human beings in the coming year.

The men, women, and children are neatly dressed. Some people wear white garments as a sign of purity. Others do not wear leather shoes, cosmetics, or perfume as a sign of denying themselves earthly comforts. For the past 24 hours, the worshippers have fasted.

Jews around the world gather to observe Yom Kippur.

THE HEBREW LANGUAGE

The Hebrew language is the language of ancient Israel and the Hebrew Bible. Because it is the language of holy texts, Hebrew is considered sacred—the language of God. It is a Semitic language closely related to Aramaic and Arabic and extinct languages such as Phoenician and Moabite. The Hebrew language has changed significantly from biblical times to the present, evolving in both its written and spoken forms. For example, during the Middle Ages, from roughly the 400s to the 1200s CE, Hebrew borrowed many words from Spanish, Greek, and Arabic.

Millions of people worldwide speak Modern Hebrew. The Hebrew alphabet has 22 letters. Unlike English, Hebrew is written and read from right to left. There are several types of Hebrew script, including the familiar block letters used in Jewish holy texts. The English language has borrowed many Hebrew words. The word *cider* comes from the Hebrew *shekar*, meaning "strong drink." *Cherub* is the English word for the Hebrew *keruv*, used in the Bible for an angel or messenger from heaven. Modern Hebrew is one of two official languages of Israel, the other being Arabic.

They have neither eaten nor drunk. They have given up food to show their sadness over committing sins, freeing themselves to focus only on their prayers.

Since the previous evening, the congregation has recited a series of confessional prayers. In these prayers, spoken in the Hebrew language, the worshippers confess their sins and ask for God's forgiveness and mercy as he judges them for the New Year. Will God seal their names in the Book of Life? Yom Kippur is each worshipper's final chance to repent before God makes this judgment.

A cantor or a rabbi—a religious teacher—leads some prayers. A few prayers are spoken aloud, while others are read silently from a prayer book. Sometimes, the whole congregation chants a prayer together. Some prayers are said while standing and others while sitting.

Some believe the shofar's blast helps humble those who hear it.

As darkness approaches, signaling the end of praying time, Yom Kippur reaches its climax. The praying becomes louder and more intense. The doors to the Holy Ark, an ornamental closet that contains the synagogue's holy scrolls, are opened. Everyone rises and begins to recite the prayer neilah, meaning "closing of the gates." It is the last chance to plead with God.

Outside the synagogue windows, the sun has set and the stars are out. At this moment, the peak of the congregants' prayer and devotion, everyone sings out together the centerpiece of Jewish prayer, the Shema: "Hear O Israel, the Lord is our God, the Lord is One."[1] Soon afterward, the shofar is blown in a long, triumphant blast, announcing the end of Yom Kippur. The worshippers rejoice, trusting their prayers will be answered. They return home to break their fast with a family meal.

What Is Judaism?

Judaism is one of the world's major religions. The term *Judaism*, however, refers to more than just a belief in a specific set of religious ideas. It also encompasses the history and practices of the Jewish people across thousands of years and includes their customs and writings, both religious and secular.

The core belief of Judaism is the existence of one God who created people and the world. It is monotheistic, believing in a single creator-God. The Jewish people rely on the Torah—a collection of Jewish holy books—as a source of spiritual guidance and moral law.

Judaism as it is practiced today originated between 70 CE and 500 CE. But it has roots in a national religion of a people known as the Israelites from approximately 1,000 BCE. Though smaller

THE SHEMA

The Shema is considered the central statement of Judaism. It is a declaration of both the Jewish religion and the belief in one God. The Shema is taken from the biblical Book of Deuteronomy, written in the 600s BCE. In Hebrew, the prayer begins, *"Shema Yisrael Adonai Eloheinu Adonai Echad,"* which means "Hear O Israel, the Lord is our God, the Lord is One."[2] Jews recite the Shema during the morning and the evening prayers, on holidays, on the Sabbath when the Torah is removed from the Holy Ark, and traditionally as the last words upon death, among other times.

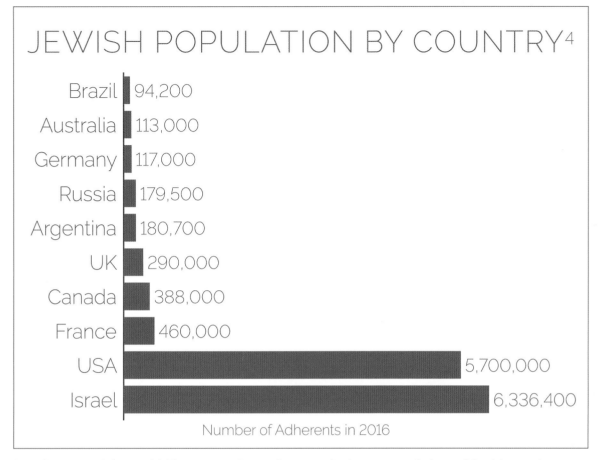

JEWISH POPULATION BY COUNTRY[4]

Country	Number of Adherents in 2016
Brazil	94,200
Australia	113,000
Germany	117,000
Russia	179,500
Argentina	180,700
UK	290,000
Canada	388,000
France	460,000
USA	5,700,000
Israel	6,336,400

Jews live around the world. These countries are home to the largest populations of Jewish people.

than other major religions—there are approximately 14 million Jews around the world—Judaism has had an enormous impact on world civilization.[3] It provided the foundation of Christianity and influenced Islam, two other monotheistic belief systems that came from the Middle East. In addition, its Ten Commandments, a set of celebrated principles regarding worship and ethics, have helped guide human behavior and have shaped humanity's philosophy for thousands of years.

A Diverse Family

Jews are members of a large family scattered around the globe. Many Jewish people live in major cities such as Tel Aviv, Israel; New York City, New York; and Chicago, Illinois. Smaller communities of Jews live in China, India, Africa, and Siberia in far-eastern Russia.

Jewish people speak and pray in many different languages. They eat different foods and wear different clothing. Jews around the world also practice Judaism differently. Customs and rituals vary, and interpretations of Jewish holy writings also differ.

This diverse mix of peoples is bound together by a sense of kinship

Some Jews live and worship in India.

and worldwide community. To Jews across the globe, the question about whether Judaism is a religion, a culture, a race, or a nationality is relatively unimportant. Judaism is largely defined by how Jewish people live.

Elements of Jewish life, including debate, introspection, the nature of God, Jewish law, and holy writings, have long been practiced within Judaism. The question "Who is a Jew?" often arises. According to Jewish law, any person born to a Jewish mother or who has converted to Judaism is a Jew.

People born Jews who reject the religion of Judaism may nevertheless consider themselves Jews, as may the Jewish community at large. Some Jews assert they are secular, or nonreligious, but take part in activities such as celebrating Jewish festivals or observing the Sabbath, or Shabbat, the seventh day of the week, from Friday evening to Saturday evening. The Torah says no work may be performed during this time, nor should a person use money, drive, or even write. Instead, the time should be spent praying to God, studying sacred writings, and spending time with loved ones.

Other Jews don't practice any aspect of Judaism at all. For such individuals, calling themselves Jews has little to do with their beliefs. Some of these people consider themselves Jewish without Judaism. For them, belonging to the Jewish community and sharing a common history is sufficient and rewarding enough to bind them to their diverse family.

ORIGINS AND FOUNDATIONS

The precise origin of Judaism is unknown. According to tradition, its roots trace back to the region known as Mesopotamia in present-day Iraq, Turkey, Syria, and Kuwait. Traditional stories tell how Judaism began with Abraham. He came from the city of Ur, located in southern Mesopotamia approximately 140 miles (225 km) southeast of the ancient city of Babylon.[1]

Father of a People

According to the Hebrew Bible, God instructed Abraham and his family to leave their native land and journey to an unknown one. In exchange, God promised Abraham that his descendants would become a great nation. Trusting in God, Abraham obeyed and

When Abraham left his native land, he took everything he had.

eventually settled in Canaan, now Israel. The people already living in the region, the Canaanites, worshipped many gods, a practice called polytheism.

Over time, Abraham developed a strong, personal relationship with God. The two entered into a covenant in which God promised to show Abraham and his descendants his favor in exchange for their faith and obedience to his laws. He commanded Abraham and his descendants to circumcise, or cut off the foreskin of, every male in their households and every baby boy eight days after birth. God also promised to give the land of Canaan to Abraham and his descendants as a homeland. Having been selected from among all other peoples on Earth to be granted God's favor, the Hebrews—the name given to Abraham's descendants—believed they were God's chosen people. To this day, the Jews have a deep attachment to both the covenant and the land of Israel. The word *Hebrew* in the Hebrew language is *Ivrie*.

Abraham was the first of three generations of biblical patriarchs, the fathers of the Hebrew people. The others were Abraham's descendants: his son Isaac and Isaac's son Jacob. God later changed Jacob's name to Israel. The Hebrews prospered and grew in numbers while living in Canaan. Their belief in one God cast them as outsiders in the eyes of the Canaanites—a perception that would haunt the Jewish people throughout the millennia.

Bondage in Egypt

Israel had 12 sons, one of them named Joseph. From the 12 sons came 12 tribes of Israel, the Israelites. According to tradition, Joseph's brothers sold him into slavery in Egypt. Joseph's character and God-given ability to interpret dreams eventually led him to a prominent position in the Egyptian pharaoh's house. Then, a devastating famine struck Canaan. Joseph had prepared Egypt for the famine, so he brought his family to the region. A few hundred years passed, and Israel's descendants multiplied in Egypt until the Hebrews numbered roughly 600,000 people. The pharaoh feared the Hebrews had become too numerous, so he enslaved them.

God sent ten plagues to Egypt, causing the pharaoh to let the Hebrews leave Egypt under the leadership of Moses. The story of their liberation is known as the Exodus, an important event in Jewish history still celebrated by Jews today. After their departure from Egypt, Moses led the Hebrews to Mount Sinai in the desert wilderness.

THE MANY NAMES OF THE HEBREW GOD

The Hebrew Bible usually calls God either Elohim or YHWH, which some people pronounce "Yahweh." The word is never pronounced by Jews as it is written but is instead replaced with the word *Adonai*, which means "Lord." Other names of God appear in Jewish scriptures, including *El* ("God") and *Ehyeh asher Ehyeh* ("I Am Who I Am").

ESCAPING EGYPT

The Jewish holiday Passover, or Pesach in Hebrew, celebrates the Exodus of the Hebrews from Egyptian slavery. The holiday lasts seven days each spring. During this time, Jews may not eat any foods made with leavening, a baking ingredient that makes dough rise. These include most products made with grain, such as wheat, rye, or oats. According to tradition, Hebrews baked unleavened bread called matzah to eat because, in their haste to flee Egypt, they did not have time to wait for their bread dough to rise.

The word *Passover* originates with the ten plagues God sent against the Egyptians. The final plague was the death of each firstborn Egyptian child. The Bible says God commanded the Hebrews to sacrifice a lamb and brush its blood on their doorframes. This would be a sign for the plague to pass over their homes.

On the first two nights of the holiday, Jews attend a Passover Seder, a festive dinner where family and friends gather to commemorate their ancestors' new freedom. Several foods symbolizing the Hebrews'

While some Seder plates have a lamb bone, others might have a bone from a different animal, such as a chicken.

captivity and escape are eaten at the dinner. Matzah, bitter herbs, and salt water, for example, signify the harshness of slavery. Eggs, fresh fruit, and vegetables symbolize freedom. Before the main meal is served, family members take turns reading from the Haggadah, a prayer book that includes a retelling of the Exodus story.

Depictions of the Ten Commandments are common in Jewish art and appear in many synagogues.

On the mountaintop, God gave Moses a set of laws by which the Hebrews were to live and worship God. These laws included the Torah—the first five books of the Hebrew Bible, also called the Pentateuch. The Torah contained the Ten Commandments, which God inscribed on two stone tablets. God also promised Moses that if the Hebrews followed his laws, he would deliver them back to the land of Canaan.

Returning Home

The Hebrews did not obey God, so they spent the next 40 years wandering the desert, during which time Moses died. Under the leadership of Moses's successor, Joshua, God allowed the Hebrews to finally enter Canaan. To reclaim the land, the Hebrews fought the Canaanites in a series of bloody battles known as the Conquest. By means of military victories and treaty agreements with the Canaanites, the Hebrews gained control over most of Canaan, though they never drove out their foes entirely. Beginning at approximately this time, the Hebrews are referred to as Israelites because of their forefather Jacob's name, Israel.

Gradually, the unity of the Israelites began to weaken as individual tribes vied for territory and political influence. During this time of internal struggle, the Philistines, invaders from the Mediterranean Sea, settled on the southern seacoast of Canaan. The Philistines' powerful armies began to push the Israelites out of Canaan, and, in one battle, they captured the Ark of the Covenant, the sacred chest that contained the stone tablets of the Ten Commandments. The Israelites realized that if they did not reunite, they would be destroyed.

God told the prophet Samuel to name a king to unite the Israelites. In approximately 1020 BCE, Samuel chose a man named Saul to be the first unifier and king of the Israelites. Though Saul did not succeed in building a solid union among the tribes, he achieved moderate success against the Philistines. In roughly 1000 BCE, David, a former shepherd and soldier, replaced Saul as king.

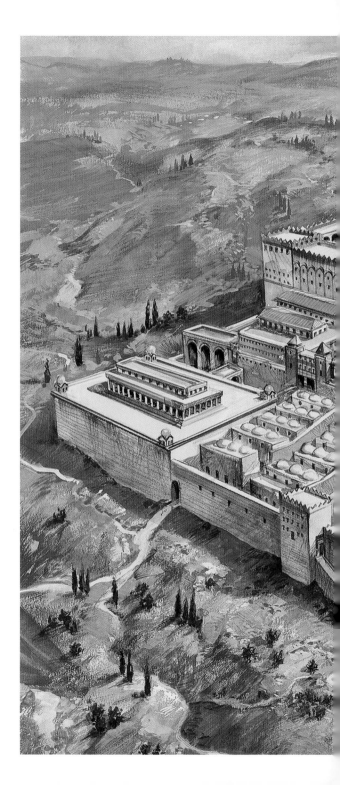

Solomon's Temple, *center*, stood on the Temple Mount, a Jewish holy place.

The House of David

Leading a powerful army, David seized the ancient fortress city of Jerusalem from a Canaanite tribe and made it the capital of his new government. The Israelites conquered new territories, expanding their borders farther north and east. David recaptured the Ark of the Covenant and brought it to the capital, a symbolic and spiritual triumph for the Israelites.

David wanted to have a close, personal relationship with God. According to ancient Jewish tradition, he wrote much of the Book of Psalms, part of the Hebrew Bible. In these writings, readers learn the writer's desire to develop such a relationship. The most familiar of the writings, Psalm 23, begins, "The Lord is my shepherd, I shall not want."[2]

David's successor, his son Solomon, is best remembered as the builder of the First Temple in Jerusalem. According to non-biblical historical sources, it was finished in 957 BCE. Non-biblical sources better determine precise dates than biblical accounts. Eventually, the elaborate, magnificently

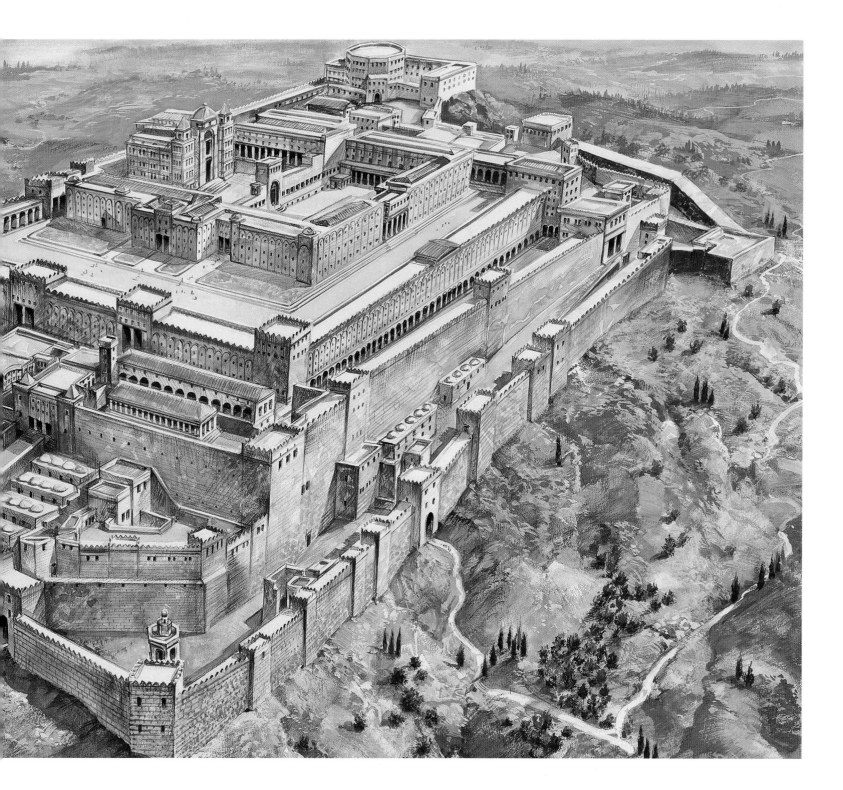

decorated structure became the only official place where Israelites could make sacrifices to God. People offered animal sacrifices and food offerings to atone for their sins, the ways they had broken God's law. Construction of the Temple, however, contributed to a split among the tribes. The northern ten tribes of Israel were heavily taxed to pay for the Temple and other projects built in the South. In addition, the northern tribes were indignant because Kings David and Solomon belonged to the tribe of Judah, one of the two southern tribes.

After Solomon died in approximately 925 BCE, the northern tribes split from the monarchy and established the Kingdom of Israel. The South became the Kingdom of Judah. In 721 BCE, the Assyrians, who controlled Mesopotamia, conquered Israel. The victors exiled much of the population of the Kingdom of Israel, scattering it throughout the region. The ten displaced northern tribes are called the Lost Tribes of Israel. They were absorbed by the regions they were sent to, disappearing.

In 587 BCE, Judah faced a different foe. The Babylonians, from present-day Iraq, overran Jerusalem. The Babylonians destroyed the Temple and deported many people of Judah to places throughout the Babylonian Empire. The event, known as the Exile, had a powerful and lasting impact on Judaism.

At this point, the Israelites became commonly known as Jews. The term *Jew* is derived from the word *Yehudi*, meaning "from the Tribe of Judah" or "from the Kingdom of Judah." Without the Temple where they could perform animal sacrifices to God, the Jews in exile came to believe that God could be worshipped anywhere. The faith in one supreme God would continue by studying the sacred texts. During the years of exile, religious scholars wrote down the history of the Jewish people and the teachings about religion and God. In time, rabbis and religious scholars replaced the priests of the Temple.

Return to Jerusalem

In 539 BCE, the Persians conquered the Babylonian Empire, including Judah, which was renamed Judea. King Cyrus of Persia allowed the Jewish exiles to return home. The Jews completed the construction of the Second Temple in 515 BCE.

Under Ezra, a Jewish priest and scribe, and Nehemiah, a devoted Jew who held a high position in the Persian court, the Torah became the law of the land in Judea. Observing the Sabbath was strictly enforced. Together, the Torah and the Temple provided Judaism with structure to continue worshipping God in its traditional ways.

RABBINIC JUDAISM

To preserve Jewish identity and ideology during the Babylonian Exile, a form of Judaism called rabbinic Judaism slowly emerged. Rabbis accomplished these goals by creating many new laws, rules, and traditions. The rabbis believed God revealed the Torah to Moses in two forms, the written law and the oral law. The rabbis produced many different texts introducing and interpreting the oral tradition. Rabbinic Judaism blossomed after the Roman destruction of the Second Temple in 70 CE and the subsequent scattering of Jews into communities around the world.

The Greek Period

After Alexander the Great conquered the Persians in 332 BCE, Judea became part of the Greek Empire. For many years, the Jews of Judea retained much religious freedom and were permitted to govern themselves by the laws of the Torah.

However, the Greeks eventually began persecuting the Jews. The Greeks tried to make all their subjects like Greeks, so they defiled the Temple, destroyed copies of the Torah, and outlawed the Jewish Sabbath and circumcision.

Many Jews resisted the Greeks' repression. One family of Jewish priests, the Maccabees, waged an armed revolt against their foes, resulting in the recapture of the Temple in 164 BCE. Today, Jews celebrate the event at the annual festival Hanukkah.

The Romans and Dispersion

The Romans seized control of Judea in 37 BCE. Herod, a Jew by birth, became king with the backing of Roman leaders. Known as Herod the Great, he was a master builder, erecting major cities and fortresses, such as the one at Masada. To win over his Jewish subjects, Herod expanded the Temple.

After Herod's death in 4 BCE, governors under direct Roman administration ruled Judea. Suppression of Jewish life increased, resulting in outbreaks of protests and armed confrontations with Roman soldiers. A full-scale Jewish rebellion erupted in 66 CE, but stronger Roman forces crushed it.

THE SIEGE AT MASADA

Herod the Great built the fortress of Masada between 37 and 31 BCE as a refuge. It stands on a tall rock cliff at the western end of the Judean Desert near the Dead Sea. During the Jewish revolt against the Romans in 66 CE, Jewish rebels overran Roman soldiers at Masada and took control of the fortress. The first-century-CE historian Josephus documented the event. After the destruction of the Jerusalem Temple in 70 CE, more rebels and their families fled to the desert to join their comrades at Masada. For years, the Jewish fighters repelled Roman attempts to seize the fortress. In the end, nearly 1,000 Jews took their last stand against Roman domination. Josephus says that, facing eventual defeat, the Jews and their families committed suicide rather than be taken prisoner.

Josephus's account of the suicides is a hotly debated topic. Some people say the mass suicide never happened; others say archaeological evidence proves it is historical fact. Archaeologists have discovered 25 skeletons in a cave on the southern cliff of the fortress.[3] Did these people commit suicide, or did the Romans kill them? What of the hundreds of other people whose remains have never been found? Unless more evidence surfaces, historians may never know the true fate of the Jews at Masada.

In 70 CE, the Romans conquered Jerusalem and destroyed the Temple. They killed tens of thousands of Jews in Jerusalem and other parts of the empire, and they sold thousands more into slavery. The Jewish state ceased to exist. In 135 CE, the Romans banned the practice of Judaism entirely. Hundreds of thousands of Jews were enslaved or killed.

Their homeland destroyed, most remaining Jews moved away. The scattering of the Jewish people around the world came to be known as the Diaspora. This means "dispersion" in Greek. It would be nearly 2,000 years until the Jews would reclaim their ancestral homeland.

INTO THE MODERN ERA

After the Roman destruction of the Second Temple in 70 CE, Jews spread to all points in the civilized world. Jewish communities were established throughout Europe, the Middle East, North Africa, and even as far away as India and China. The Diaspora helped Jewish culture survive yet also threatened the existence of the Jewish people.

Divisions within Judaism

The scattering of the Jewish population throughout Europe created two major religious-cultural divisions within Judaism: Sephardim and Ashkenazim. The Sephardim originated in the Iberian Peninsula, which includes Spain and Portugal. Sephardic (meaning "Iberian" in Hebrew) Jews spoke Ladino, a blend of Spanish and Hebrew. When Islamic armies conquered the region in the early 700s, many Jews from other points in Europe migrated westward to Iberia. The Jewish

Some early Sephardic manuscripts have been preserved, including one showing a Jewish family during Passover.

community grew and prospered under Muslim rule. Jews often served in official government capacities and made important contributions to Muslim Arab culture. Many Sephardic Jews spoke Arabic, and Jewish religious texts were frequently written in that language.

The Jews of central Europe became known as Ashkenazic Jews. The first Ashkenazic community appeared in present-day western Germany. Other large communities sprang up in Poland, Hungary, and Lithuania. The Ashkenazim developed the Yiddish language, a form of German that incorporates Hebrew words.

The Sephardim and Ashkenazim share the common bonds of Judaism but differ in many respects. In addition to speaking different languages, the two groups pronounce Hebrew differently. Prayers are slightly different, and the foods of each culture differ because they originated in different countries. Traditionally, the Ashkenazim concentrated more on the study of religion and Jewish law than the Sephardim, who more fully embraced science and secular philosophy.

Mistreatment and Persecution

Over the centuries, the degree to which Diaspora Jews enjoyed religious freedom in their newfound homelands ebbed and flowed. Whether in Europe, North Africa, or the Middle East, Jews experienced periods of both prosperity and persecution.

The roots of anti-Semitism, or anti-Jewish sentiment, can be traced back nearly 2,000 years. At that time, many leaders of the Catholic Church established the pattern of anti-Semitism that exists to

HASIDISM

In the mid-1700s in eastern Europe, a movement known as Hasidism blossomed in response to rabbinic Judaism's scholarly approach to Jewish scriptures. Led by charismatic Rabbi Ba'al Shem Tov ("Master of the Good Name of God"), Hasidism promoted the concept that Jews should establish strong emotional connections with God through joyful experiences—high-spirited dancing, singing, storytelling, and intense, ecstatic prayer. The movement appealed to the poor and less-educated Jews of the region who wished to find a simpler, less intellectual approach to Judaism. By the early 1800s, a significant portion of religious Jews in eastern Europe had adopted Hasidism.

After the Holocaust and the destruction of eastern European towns during World War II (1939–1945), many Hasidic communities relocated to Israel and the United States. The two largest groups, the Lubavitcher and the Satmar, are headquartered in Brooklyn, New York City. Traditionally, Hasidim wear distinctive clothing and hats. Men generally have beards and dress in black suits or three-quarter-length black coats. Women wear modest, loose-fitting dresses with wigs covering their hair.

this day. Official church doctrine said the Jews killed Jesus Christ, whom Christians believe is the Son of God, and that both the destruction of the Second Temple and the Diaspora were God's punishments for past misdeeds. Furthermore, the church portrayed the Jews as evil outsiders and troublemakers because they failed to accept Christianity.

Numerous myths further fanned the flames of anti-Semitism. The myth of blood libel—that Jews used the blood of Christian children in religious rituals—was widely accepted as truth, as were claims that Jews poisoned the drinking waters in Christian communities. Many Christians viewed the Jews' failure to convert to Christianity as a sign of serving the Antichrist, the sinister figure in the New Testament who opposes Christ when Christ returns to fulfill God's prophecies.

Fueled by such perceptions, violence against Jews was not uncommon. In 1096, Christian crusaders set out on long journeys to fight Muslims in the Holy Land, which used to belong to the Kingdom of Judah. As the crusaders passed through Jewish villages on the way, they slaughtered thousands of Jews because the Jews refused to convert. The armies killed even more Jews in France and Germany in later crusades.

Many Christian leaders blamed Jews for the Black Death that killed millions of Europeans during the 1300s. Taken as scapegoats for the deadly plague, the Jews became the victims of massacres and persecution.

The crusaders killed many Jews at Metz, a city in France.

Jewish homes and businesses were destroyed, and many Jews were murdered, including hundreds of Jews who were burned alive in Strasbourg, France.

Removals, Ghettos, and Pogroms

In 1290, the Jews were expelled from England, and then from France in 1306. In 1492, following years of severe persecution, King Ferdinand and Queen Isabella of Spain ordered their country's Jews to convert to Christianity or be killed. Some 200,000 Jews fled Spain, settling mainly in Morocco, Greece, the Netherlands, Turkey, and Italy. Others relocated to large cities in northwestern Europe, such as London, England, where they were allowed again. In 1569, Pope Pius expelled all Jews from the Papal States, located in present-day Italy. Less than 30 years later, the Jews were ordered out of the rest of Italy and Bavaria, Germany.

In many places, Jews were forcibly segregated from the rest of the population. They were made to live in sections of towns called ghettos. In the 1500s and 1600s, government officials established ghettos for Jews in Rome, Italy; Frankfurt, Germany; and many other European cities. Ghetto living involved disease-ridden conditions with poor sanitation, limited food resources, and a lack of clean water.

In eastern Europe, Jews were frequently the victims of pogroms, a Russian word meaning "to demolish violently." These anti-Jewish riots occurred periodically throughout the 1800s and 1900s in Ukraine, southern Russia, Poland, and Belarus, killing tens of thousands of Jews. In many cases, government and police officials encouraged violence toward Jews and theft of Jewish property.

The Holocaust

The Holocaust occurred from 1933 to 1945. Also called the Shoah (Hebrew for "Devastation"), it was the Nazi regime's systematic, government-sponsored murder of 6 million Jews—more than one-third of all Jews living on Earth. Among those killed were 1.5 million children.[1] German dictator Adolf Hitler believed Jews represented a threat to humanity—and, more importantly, to the German nation. He blamed the Jews for corrupting morals, for the worldwide economic depression of the 1930s, and more. Hitler and his Nazi collaborators claimed Jews were a genetically inferior and criminal race that had to be extinguished. A long history of anti-Semitism inspired Hitler's actions. Dutch journalist Pierre van Paassen wrote, "I am convinced that Hitler neither could nor would have done to the Jewish people what he has done . . . if we [Christians] had not actively prepared the way for him by our own unfriendly attitude to the Jews, by our selfishness and by the anti-Semite teaching in our churches and schools."[2]

Hitler began persecuting the Jews immediately upon his election as chancellor of Germany in 1933. The Nazis enacted laws that removed Jews from public service, political office, and land ownership. Many Jews were arrested and sent to labor camps. By 1941, in the middle of World War II (1939–1945), the regime devised a plan to murder every Jew living in German-controlled lands. Tens of thousands of Jews were shot in Germany and Poland, with entire communities of Jews tortured and murdered. In many cases, anti-Semitic local populations hunted and killed Jews. Thousands of Jews were put to hard labor for the Nazis. Others were rounded up and forced to move into ghettos. There, more than 800,000 Jews are estimated to have died from disease, starvation, and murder at the hands of the Nazis.[3]

In 1942, Hitler and other German leaders established six death camps in Poland. Jews were deported from lands throughout Europe and transported to the camps in railway cars. Anyone attempting to escape was shot. At the camps, German guards sometimes herded groups of Jews into chambers, locked the doors, and filled the rooms with lethal gas. More than three million Jews were murdered at the six camps.[4]

ELIE WIESEL, HOLOCAUST SURVIVOR

Holocaust survivor Elie Wiesel was born in 1928 in present-day Romania and was raised as a Jew. At age 15, he was imprisoned at the Auschwitz death camp and was later sent to labor camps, also called concentration camps. Concentration camps held prisoners of many nationalities. Prisoners often died from hunger, disease, or physical exhaustion. Death camps, also called extermination centers, were different. Nearly all death camp prisoners were Jewish. The ultimate goal of these places was to kill Jews. The Nazis killed Wiesel's mother, father, and sister. After the war, Wiesel became a US citizen and wrote extensively about Jewish suffering in the death camps. In 1978, Wiesel was appointed head of the President's Commission on the Holocaust by President Jimmy Carter. Wiesel also spoke out in support of people who were persecuted around the world. In 1986, he received the Nobel Peace Prize. The international activist for peace died in 2016 at the age of 87.

Guards sometimes killed those too weak to stand in Nazi camps.

Founding a New Home

After Germany lost World War II, many surviving Jews returned to their villages to attempt to rebuild their lives. The returnees often found their homes looted or inhabited by strangers. Many Jews immigrated to the United States, Canada, and South America. A much-desired destination was

British-controlled Palestine—the Hebrews' original homeland—where Jews from many countries had already been moving for several decades. Many of these Jews were Zionists, people who wanted to create a Jewish state and refuge for Jews.

Arabs opposed the establishment of a Jewish state in Palestine. To appease them, the British limited Jewish immigration. Armed conflict erupted between Jews living in Palestine and both the British and the Arabs. Unable to stem the violence, the British asked the United Nations (UN) to solve the problem. In 1947, the UN approved a plan to divide Palestine into two states: an independent Jewish state of Israel and a Palestinian state. Arab leaders rejected the plan and launched attacks against Jewish settlers. Despite the continuing violence, on May 14, 1948, the chair of the Provisional State Council of Israel, David Ben-Gurion, proclaimed the State of Israel. This established the first Jewish state in 2,000 years.

THE ARAB-ISRAELI WAR

On May 15, 1948—one day after Israel declared itself a state—a coalition of Arab states attacked the newly formed nation. Armies from Egypt, Jordan, Iraq, Syria, and Lebanon stormed into Israel and battled Jewish forces. The war ended in March 1949, with victorious Israel in control of one-third more territory. But Arab–Israeli hostilities continued with wars fought in 1956, 1967, 1973, and 1982. Despite frequent attempts to bring about lasting peace, armed conflict between Arab factions and Israel rages to this day.

WHAT JEWS BELIEVE

Defining exactly what Jews believe is a challenging task. Throughout the millennia, Jews have worshipped and practiced in different ways. Different movements within the religion place emphasis on different beliefs.

Many Jews practice Judaism rigorously, others do not practice at all, and some even deny the existence of God yet would not hesitate to proclaim they are Jews. While there is no absolute concept of Judaism, several traditional beliefs provide the foundation of modern Judaism.

God

Judaism is based on monotheism. The God of the Jews is all powerful and invisible. God stands above and outside his creation. He is omnipresent, which means he is always everywhere. God is good and

Jews of many practices pray at the Western Wall, the last remaining section of the Second Temple.

37

PERSPECTIVES

THIRTEEN PRINCIPLES OF FAITH

Moses Maimonides was the leading Torah scholar and Jewish philosopher of the late 1100s CE. Maimonides believed there were 13 basic principles of Judaism. Those principles are:

1. God is the creator and ruler of all things.

2. God is one.

3. God does not have a body.

4. God is eternal.

5. God is the only power worthy of our prayers.

6. God has revealed his will through the prophets.

7. Moses is the greatest prophet.

8. The Torah, God's revelation, was given directly to Moses.

9. The Torah is eternal truth and cannot be changed.

10. God knows all of man's deeds and thoughts.

11. God rewards those who obey his commandments and punishes those who disobey him.

12. God will one day send the Messiah.

13. The dead will be brought back to life when God wishes.

caring and is the source of morality and virtue. God is one—a unified, indivisible entity.

God is transcendent, meaning beyond the range of physical human experience. God cannot be fully understood, nor can he be described in words. Though all powerful and omniscient, God does not direct all human affairs. Instead, he allows humankind to exercise free will, which God has bestowed upon humans. God is also eternal. He has always existed and always will exist. He is perfect and does not change.

God is both transcendent and unknowable, yet he is personal and approachable. These apparent contradictions

THE JEWS AS THE CHOSEN PEOPLE

The notion of chosenness originated with the Jews' covenant with God at Mount Sinai. The concept does not, nor should it, imply an innate Jewish superiority over any other religion or race. "The concept of chosen people means *not* that Jews were chosen for special privilege, but for sacred responsibility," writes Rabbi Wayne Dosick.[1]

According to biblical writings, this responsibility includes bringing God's Torah to the rest of the world. To perform this duty, Judaism teaches that Jews must strive for a higher purpose by learning, living, and teaching God's ways. Chosenness, therefore, is not about special rights, but exactly the opposite. Amos 3:2 in the Hebrew Bible explains the burden: "You [the Jewish people] alone I have singled out of all the families of the Earth—That is why I will call you to account for all your iniquities."[2]

coexist in Judaism. Though God stands above and outside his creation, he is caring and attentive, hearing and answering people's prayers.

Because God has no body, it is impossible to conceive of God as exclusively male or female. Judaism teaches God has both male and female qualities. Traditionally, God is referred to in masculine terms, such as *he*, *him*, or *Father*. However, many Jews believe it would be equally proper to use feminine words for God—*she*, *her*, or *Mother*.

The Torah and Covenants

Another cornerstone of Jewish belief is that the Torah was given directly by God to Moses on Mount Sinai. In broader interpretations, the Torah can also mean the entire Hebrew Bible, or the totality of God's revelations to the Jews—both the written Torah and the oral Torah. The Torah is the fundamental source of Jewish beliefs and practices. It teaches that human life has purpose and dignity.

Two covenants, or agreements, play a central role in Judaism: the covenant between God and

Abraham and the covenant between God and the people of Israel at Mount Sinai. These agreements

provide the basis for the enduring relationship between God and the Jews. In the first covenant,

God makes Abraham three promises: the promise of land, the promise of many descendants who

will become a great nation, and the promise that all the people on Earth would be blessed through

Jews may gather to study the Torah together and help each other learn from it.

him. In exchange, Abraham and his descendants must agree to serve God, and they symbolize that agreement with circumcision.

The second covenant with God was accepted by the Israelites when Moses received the Ten Commandments. In this agreement, God promised to make the Israelites a holy nation if they would accept and observe God's divine laws. This agreement sets Israel apart from other nations as God's chosen people. In this agreement, called the Mosaic Covenant, God will bless the Jews if they honor their commitment and obey his laws. If they are disobedient, however, God will punish them or send them into exile.

THE MESSIAH: WHO, WHAT, AND WHEN?

According to Jewish tradition, the Messiah will be a male human being, not a god or supernatural being. He will be a military-political leader descended from King David. A religious man who observes Jewish law, the Messiah will appear in a time of danger to save the Jews. It is said he will gather the Jews of the world to Israel and return them to the holy ways of the Torah. No one knows when the Messiah will arrive, but suggestions made by scholars about what could trigger the event include: if all Jews observed a single Sabbath properly, if people who fear sin become hated, or if a generation loses hope totally.

The Messiah

Traditional Judaism teaches that the Messiah, or *mashiach* in Hebrew, meaning "anointed one," will appear on Earth and lead the Jewish people to an era of unity and peace, returning to the holy ways of the Torah. The Messiah will transform the world into a paradise, a perfect place without pain or evil.

Christians believe the Messiah has already arrived in the form of Jesus Christ. Nearly all Jews who believe in the coming of the Messiah reject the idea of Jesus as the Messiah. Biblical prophecies say the Messiah will bring peace and harmony to the world. Because the world is still a place of pain and hate, Jews do not believe that the Messiah has come yet.

In addition, according to Moses Maimonides, an influential Jewish scholar from the 1100s, the Messiah would be known by accomplishing several important tasks. Among these tasks are rebuilding the Temple in Jerusalem, gathering Jews around the world to the land of Israel, and defeating Israel's enemies in battle. Maimonides wrote, "And if he's not successful with this, or if he is killed, it's known that he is not the one that was promised by the Torah."[3]

The Afterlife

Judaism does not have a single, fixed notion about life after death, often referred to as the world to come. The Torah is silent about the afterlife. Some

Maimonides was born in Cordova, Spain.

Jews don't believe in an afterlife at all. The issues of the resurrection of the dead and the immortality of the soul appear in many scholarly texts, but the writings are frequently vague and contradictory.

In biblical times, death meant rejoining one's ancestors. Another biblical mention of death and the afterlife is a shadowy place called Sheol, to which human souls go after death. In later years, the concept of resurrection of the dead began to appear in Jewish writings. Scholars presented different notions regarding how resurrection would occur, including the belief that the righteous will rise from the dead, wearing their clothes, in Jerusalem. In some writings, only the righteous will be resurrected, while others state that everyone will be resurrected, followed by a day of judgment for entry to heaven or hell.

Gan Eden, meaning "Garden of Eden," is the Jewish heaven. It has been described as a place of happiness and tranquility. According to one concept, people enjoy lavish banquets, while in another, Gan Eden is described as a place where souls without bodies rest, not eating or drinking.

The concept of *Gehenom*, the Jewish hell, originated with the place called Sheol in the Bible. The unrighteous Jews will go to Gehenom after death. To some scholars, the souls of the unrighteous are punished for 12 months, but then, after cleansing and purification, they are sent to Gan Eden. In another interpretation, some sinners who never repent are sent to Gehenom and remain there for eternity in a realm described as "boiling filth."[4]

Helping people before they require charity by helping them find employment, providing a loan or gift, or helping establish them in a self-sufficient business.

Giving when neither party knows the other's identity.

Giving when the donor knows the recipient's identity, but the recipient doesn't know the donor's identity.

Giving when the recipient knows the donor's identity.

Giving without being asked.

Giving after being asked.

Giving less than one should, but giving cheerfully.

Giving begrudgingly.

According to Maimonides, there are eight levels of charity ranging from the least admirable, *bottom*, to the most admirable, *top*.

Some Jews give food to those who can't afford it as an act of charity.

Tzedakah

The Torah commands that Jews must care for the needy and the less fortunate. Tzedakah is the Hebrew word loosely translated as "charity" in English. However, the Hebrew root of the word means "justice" or "fairness." Judaism teaches that tzedakah is a righteous act and that it is the duty of every Jew to give money, worldly goods, and time to those in need.

Jews work to provide for people's long-term needs. They have built hospitals and schools. Jews may volunteer at these places or with other organizations committed to helping people. Those unable to volunteer time or work may help fund these efforts. Jews have practiced charity since biblical times. This value of caring for others has helped people around the world.

Judaism has many sacred books that provide instruction, tell stories, and help people worship.

SACRED SCRIPTURES

People who follow Judaism, as well as those who follow Christianity and Islam, are called "the People of the Book." All three religions have books considered to be written by God through people. For Jews, the book is the Hebrew Bible. The faithful study of this Bible has always been a core element of Judaism. Collectively, these writings are known as the Jewish Scriptures, the divinely inspired words of God.

The Tanakh

Traditionally, the Hebrew Bible has been known by several different names. Today, it is called the Tanakh, a word formed by combining the Hebrew first letters of each of its three parts: the Torah, Nevi'im (Prophets), and Ketuvim (Writings).

WOMEN AND THE TORAH

The Book of Genesis, the first book of the Hebrew Bible, says, "And God created man in His Image, in the image of God He created him: male and female He created them."[1] Some Jewish scholars interpret this passage to mean Adam was both male and female, and was later separated. Both sexes were created equally and were equal in the eyes of God.

The Bible contains many stories of powerful and intelligent women, such as Sarah and Rebecca, and the prophetesses Miriam, Deborah, and Yael. Some biblical women also held positions of authority. Frequently, however, women are portrayed as inferior to men in the Bible. Genesis 3:16 states that, as a result of sin entering the world, man would rule over woman. The Book of Leviticus declares that women were not allowed to be priests. In Numbers 30:3–6, if a man made a vow or took an oath, "he must carry out all that has crossed his lips."[2] A vow by a woman, however, could be canceled by her father.

Negative attitudes toward women in the Bible reflect the male-dominated societies when scriptures were written. Though having a vital role in the home and in the family, women held few legal rights and were subordinate to men in nearly all aspects of ancient society.

The Torah consists of Genesis, Exodus, Leviticus, Numbers, and Deuteronomy. Judaism teaches that the Torah, the Hebrew word for "law," contains Judaism's most important guiding principles. It is a narrative, beginning with the creation of the universe and ending with the death of Moses, just prior to the Jews' passage into Canaan. The Torah, however, is not merely a historical account of the early Jews but also a guide to worshipping God. Leviticus, the third book of the Torah, includes sets of laws telling Jews which foods they may and may not eat. A large portion of Leviticus reveals the rewards for obeying God's words and the punishments for failing to obey.

The Nevi'im makes up the second part of the Tanakh. It is composed of eight books: Joshua, Judges, Samuel, Kings, Isaiah, Jeremiah, Ezekiel, and the Twelve Minor Prophets. Historically, the Nevi'im begins with the Conquest of Israel by Joshua and ends with prophecies of rebuilding the Temple after the Jews' return from the Babylonian Exile.

In biblical times, the primary role of the prophet was usually not to predict the future. Instead, prophets tried to change and improve society by encouraging people to follow God's commandments. Historically, prophets also advised Jewish rulers. These functions could involve forecasting the future, but prophets were more often God's message bearers to the Israelites, especially in times of crisis and upheaval.

JEWISH DIETARY LAWS

The Hebrew Bible lists the kinds of foods that may or may not be eaten by Jews. These dietary laws are called kashrut. Foods that may be consumed are said to be kosher. Nonkosher foods are called *trayf*. There are several main rules. Only animals with split hooves that chew their cud, such as cattle, sheep, and goats, are kosher. All other animals with split hooves, such as pigs, are not. Only seafood with scales and fins may be eaten. Shellfish—such as lobsters, shrimp, and clams—are forbidden. Reptiles, some insects, and amphibians are trayf. Milk and meat may not be consumed during the same meal. No animal's blood may be eaten. Animals must be killed in a specified manner by draining the blood and washing the meat. Chickens, turkeys, ducks, and other domesticated birds are kosher. Birds of prey, such as eagles, falcons, hawks, and buzzards, are trayf.

The final portion of the Tanakh, the Ketuvim, is a collection of 14 books of literature, including love songs, history, wisdom, and poetry. Psalms is a series of songs of praise to God. Proverbs offers sayings to help guide people in their everyday lives. Lamentations commemorates the destruction of the First Temple. In dramatic poetry, the book recounts the ruination of Jerusalem and the exile that followed.

The Mishnah

Judaism teaches that God gave Moses two sets of laws on Mount Sinai: the written law (the Torah) and the oral law, which contained additional commandments from God. For hundreds of years, rabbis taught these laws orally. After more than one million Jews—including many biblical scholars—were killed by the Romans during Jewish revolts in the first century CE, the rabbis decided to write down the oral law to prevent it from being lost forever.

Between 200 and 220 CE, Rabbi Judah ha-Nasi, or Judah the Prince, collected the oral laws and their interpretations by rabbis in a book called the Mishnah. The Mishnah is divided into six sections, each one primarily devoted to a different subject. This legal commentary offers rabbinic opinions on many aspects of Jewish life, from agricultural matters to Jewish civil and criminal law, observance of religious holidays, marriage and divorce, and matters of ethics. The Mishnah's rulings about civil law, marriage relations, and the celebration of holidays and festivals remain valid to this day and serve as a guiding tool in contemporary Jewish life.

The Talmud

The Mishnah provides the foundation for the most important sacred text in Judaism after the Torah—the Talmud. For the next 400 years after the Mishnah was completed, Jewish scholars studied and discussed the text. They debated its contents and other legal and social issues at Jewish learning academies in Palestine and Babylon. Eventually, these discussions were carefully edited into a work called the Gemara. The Mishnah and the Gemara together form the Talmud. Each academy produced its own version of the Talmud, although they share common material.

The Palestinian Talmud, also known as the Jerusalem Talmud, was completed in approximately 425 CE, while the Babylonian Talmud was finished by 500 CE. The Babylonian

THE 613 COMMANDMENTS

The Talmud says there are 613 commandments in the Torah but does not list them. Over the centuries, there have been many attempts to produce a list of the commandments. Moses Maimonides produced the most widely accepted accounting of the commandments in his *Mishneh Torah*, written between 1170 and 1180. Among the 248 positive commandments, meaning they tell readers what to do, are instructions to love and fear God, to love other Jews, to learn the Torah, to observe the Sabbath, and to give to charity. The 365 negative commandments, which tell readers what not to do, include directives not to make or worship idols, tattoo the skin, insult or harm anybody with words, or engage in astrology.[3]

A Talmud Page

- Mishnah and Gemara
- Rashi Commentary
- Other Commentaries Including Tosafot

A Talmud page can seem confusing for those unfamiliar with it. Each page has text from the Mishnah and Gemara, as well as several commentaries.

Talmud gained wider distribution and acceptance and today is considered the more authoritative text of the two.

Composed of many volumes, the Talmud records the rabbis' and scholars' conversations and debates. It also includes folktales, legends, medical advice, sermons, and more. The Talmud is a cornerstone of Jewish knowledge and tradition. Though not regarded as being divinely inspired, it has influenced other forms of Jewish culture, such as philosophy and literature, and has helped mold the Jewish people into a nation.

The Midrash

Rabbis also wrote the Midrash, a series of stories and interpretations primarily focusing on the Hebrew Bible. The word *midrash* comes from the verb *darash*, which means "to explore" or "to investigate." The rabbis carefully examined biblical texts and produced line-by-line commentaries and interpretations of them, often including fanciful tales from which to draw ethical lessons.

The goal of their work was to provide spiritual insight into the texts and provide a religious and ethical guide for future generations of Jews. There are two forms of midrash. Halachic midrash attempts to explain vague Jewish laws found in the Torah, while Aggadic midrash generally explores the lives of biblical characters.

In some synagogues, men and women may be divided by a line down the center of the sanctuary.

CHAPTER SIX

DIFFERENT VOICES: THE BRANCHES OF JUDAISM

With a worldwide Jewish population of roughly 14 million people, it's not surprising that all Jews do not practice Judaism the same way. Various Jewish sects and movements developed as early as the first century CE. Today, there are four main subdivisions, or branches, of Judaism: Orthodox, Reform, Conservative, and Reconstructionist.

Orthodox Judaism

Orthodox Judaism is grounded in traditional Jewish laws and customs. Orthodox Jews believe they are obligated to observe the written law and oral law given to Moses by God on Mount Sinai. This Jewish law—the will of God—cannot be adapted or changed to fit the times or personal whims of the individual. Orthodox Jews believe they are the only group that practices Judaism faithfully.

In Orthodox practice, men and women are prohibited from sitting together in the synagogue, where prayers are said only in Hebrew. Rabbis must be men. Many Orthodox men wear a head covering at all times. Jewish dietary laws are strictly observed. Orthodox Judaism embraces the coming of the Messiah, a rebuilt Temple in Jerusalem, and the resurrection of the dead. Most Orthodox Jews have a positive view of technology and scientific advances and maintain close contact with the modern world without compromising their traditional Jewish beliefs and practices. Politically, Orthodox Jews tend to be Zionists, supporting the Jewish home in the land of Israel.

There are a wide variety of practices and beliefs within the Orthodox tradition. Several branches have developed from Orthodoxy. Some ultraorthodox branches, such as the Hasidim, place studying the Torah and Talmud above all other religious and social practices. They maintain the most rigid interpretations of Jewish law. Hasidim discourage involvement in any secular activities and strive to avoid contact with modern society as much as possible. Some groups tend to be strongly anti-Zionist, asserting that only the Messiah can bring about a Jewish homeland in Israel.

Reform Judaism

Reform Judaism began in Germany in the early 1800s. The spread of the Enlightenment—a movement that celebrated human reason and the quest for freedom and equality—resulted in greater liberties

THE RISE OF ZIONISM

Zionism is a political and cultural movement that began in the late 1800s. The movement called for the establishment of a permanent Jewish homeland in Eretz Israel, the land believed by Jews to be that which God promised to Abraham and his descendants. The Jews' quest for an independent homeland was spurred by centuries of persecution and Diaspora.

Theodor Herzl, a Jewish journalist from Austria, was among the earliest proponents of a return to Eretz Israel. Herzl's *Der Judenstaat* (The Jews' State), a pamphlet published in 1896, encouraged Russian and European Jews to buy land in Palestine. Herzl argued that Jews could avoid discrimination in Europe by having their own independent Jewish state.

Even before Israel declared independence in 1948, Zionism came under attack. Many anti-Zionists, including several Arab nations, oppose a Jewish state in the Jews' ancestral homeland. Many question Israel's legal and historical rights to the land. Terrorist attacks on Zionists occur regularly in Israel despite decades of peace negotiations between the Israeli government, opposition countries, and political groups.

for European Jews. With the doors of social and political acceptance now more widely opened, these Jews hoped to bring traditional Jewish religious practices more in line with modern German society. Their goal was to become more German without losing their Jewish identity.

To accomplish this goal, they reformed Judaism by adopting new practices and eliminating beliefs that might have been perceived as superstitious and threatening by non-Jews. Reform Jews prayed in German or in the local languages as the movement spread, rather than in Hebrew. Organ music and choirs, staples of traditional Christian worship, were introduced into religious services. Reform Jews rejected dietary laws, claiming them to be outdated and unnecessary. Most rejected the concept of the Messiah bringing the Jews back to Israel and reestablishing the Temple.

Hasidic men often wear black hats and long coats and grow a lock of hair on both sides of their heads. Women often wear skirts below the knee and sleeves past the elbow, and married women may cover their hair.

Over time, Reform Judaism restored some of the practices it first rejected, abandoning many of its nontraditional beliefs and practices. The Reform movement has flourished in the United States. Today, approximately 35 percent of all American Jews belong to Reform Judaism.[1] Many people belonging to Reform Judaism are Zionists.

Conservative Judaism

Conservative Judaism arose in response to the extreme measures of the Reform movement. From its roots in the 1800s in Germany, Conservative Judaism tried to find a middle ground between Orthodox Judaism and Reform Judaism. The movement looked to preserve Jewish tradition while living in the modern world.

The Conservative movement teaches that Jewish laws, beliefs, and texts must be modified to suit the times without abandoning the core beliefs

JUDAISM AND LGBTQ PEOPLE

Within Judaism are differing attitudes regarding LGBTQ acceptance. Reform Judaism opposes discrimination against LGBTQ individuals. Guided by the belief that all human beings are created equal, LGBTQ people may be ordained as rabbis and cantors in Reform Judaism, and rabbis are permitted to perform same-sex marriages. Within Orthodox Judaism are different degrees of acceptance. While most Orthodox rabbis reject sex reassignment surgery, cross-dressing, and hormonal treatments, some Orthodox synagogues welcome LGBTQ individuals into their communities. In Conservative Judaism, gay and lesbian rabbis can be ordained, but not all Conservative rabbis will perform same-sex weddings.

Some women serve as rabbis in Germany.

of Judaism and the teachings of the Torah. Conservative Judaism accepts the divine origin of the Torah, but unlike Orthodox Judaism, it debates how it was created. Some Conservative scholars claim God wrote the Torah, while others say it was divinely inspired. A third group believes humans wrote the Torah based on their interpretation of God's intention. These differing opinions mean members hold a wide range of religious beliefs.

Conservative theology includes a belief in Torah rituals and the observance of the Sabbath and dietary laws, but it permits considerable flexibility and freedom in carrying out these responsibilities. Many Conservative Jews will admit they do not keep kosher. They may attend Sabbath services, but they might drive to the synagogue, a practice forbidden by traditional law. Women can be rabbis. Once critics of Zionism, most Conservative Jews currently support the State of Israel.

Reconstructionist Judaism

Reconstructionist Judaism, the newest and smallest branch of Judaism, originated in the United States. Founded in 1922 by Conservative rabbi Mordecai Kaplan, the movement viewed Judaism as an "evolving civilization," which involves beliefs, rituals, language, history, and other forms of

MORDECAI KAPLAN, FOUNDER OF RECONSTRUCTIONIST JUDAISM

Mordecai Kaplan was born in 1881 in Lithuania. When he was eight, his family immigrated to the United States. There, he was ordained a rabbi at the Jewish Theological Seminary, of the Conservative movement, in 1902. Learning about sociology led Kaplan to view Judaism not as a religion but as an evolving religious civilization. His 1934 book, *Judaism as a Civilization*, became the foundation of the new Reconstructionist movement. Kaplan did not view God as a supernatural entity but rather as a force that emerged from the good deeds performed by humankind. Kaplan died in 1983 at the age of 102.

Some Reconstructionists emphasize care for the environment. The Jewish Reconstructionist Congregation in Evanston, Illinois, uses energy-efficient heating and cooling as well as recycled materials.

culture.[2] Reconstructionist Judaism teaches that the religion requires occasional updating to maintain its vitality and relevance.

Reconstructionist theology breaks from mainstream Jewish thinking in several ways. Reconstructionists reject the notion of the chosenness of the Jewish people, instead saying all people can build a close relationship with God. They also deny that the Torah was revealed to the Jews at Mount Sinai. Instead, Reconstructionists say that Jewish laws and practices developed over many centuries and continue to develop to the present.

Having emerged from the Conservative movement, Reconstructionist Judaism still embraces the study of Jewish texts, observance of dietary laws, prayer in Hebrew, and men wearing head coverings in the synagogue. Reconstructionist Judaism is arguably the most inclusive branch of Judaism, as it welcomes men, women, and LGBTQ people alike. Reconstructionists were the first Jews to recognize that a child is Jewish if either the mother or father is Jewish. Traditional Jewish belief says that a person is a Jew if the mother is Jewish, regardless of the father's religion. But no matter which branch of Judaism one follows, the synagogue is the center for all Jewish worship.

THE SYNAGOGUE

Throughout Jewish history, the synagogue has served as a place of prayer and study and as a meeting place for the community. In Hebrew, the synagogue is called *Bet Knesset*, meaning "house of assembly." Jews also refer to the synagogue as a shul—which is a Yiddish word—or a temple. *Synagogue* is a Greek word meaning "assembly," similar to the Hebrew term *Bet Knesset*.

Origins

Little is known regarding the precise origin of the synagogue, but some scholars believe its beginnings date to the Babylonian Exile following the destruction of the First Temple. Most experts, however, affirm that the destruction of the Second Temple in the first century CE spurred the growth of the synagogue as an important institution in Jewish life.

A synagogue's style tends to reflect styles from the time and place in which it was built.

PERSPECTIVES

THE WRITINGS OF RASHI

Rabbi Solomon ben Isaac, known as Rashi, is one of the most influential Jewish commentators on both the Hebrew Bible and the Talmud. Born in northern France in 1040, Rashi studied with rabbinic scholars in Germany.

Rashi's commentaries helped clarify and elaborate upon Jewish scriptures, adding insight to the original texts. For example, Psalm 23 of the Hebrew Bible, known as the Psalm of David, in part reads, "He [God] restores my soul; He leads me in paths of righteousness for His name's sake." According to Rashi, "my soul" means "my spirit, which has been weakened by troubles and haste." He explains "in paths of righteousness" to mean "in straight paths, so that I should not fall into the hands of my enemies."[1]

Rashi's commentaries on the Babylonian Talmud influenced all later rabbinic commentaries. Rashi pulled together the work of earlier Talmudic commentaries into one clear, organized commentary, which enabled individuals studying the Talmud to understand it without the help of a teacher.

With the Temple gone, Jews needed a place to assemble and pray. Prayer replaced animal sacrifice at the Temple, becoming the cornerstone of Jewish religious life. By the end of the first century, synagogues were common throughout the Roman Empire in places such as Rome and Alexandria, Egypt. Synagogues existed in Jerusalem even during the time of the Temple. These early places of worship were often rooms in private houses or simple structures built specially for reading scriptures and as gathering places.

The Design of the Synagogue

There is no single, official design for the synagogue. Synagogue architecture usually follows the building styles of the region and time of construction. Synagogues in China, for example, look similar to Chinese temples, while medieval synagogues in Europe are often imposing buildings similar to churches. Over the years, synagogue architecture has featured a diverse range of building styles. Inside, however, all contemporary synagogues have three main features: an ark housing the scrolls of the Torah, a desk from which to read, and a ceiling lamp hanging in front of the ark.

The Holy Ark, or Aron Kodesh, is a cupboard-like structure built into the eastern wall of the synagogue that contains the Torah scrolls, or Siphrei Torah. The scrolls are handwritten copies of the first five books of the Hebrew Bible. Inside the doors to the Holy Ark are embroidered curtains, usually made of fine velvet, which are pulled back to reveal the scrolls at specific times during the religious service. In many synagogues, two tablets representing the Ten Commandments appear above the ark. The first two words of each commandment are etched in the tablets.

The desk at which the Torah is read is called the bimah. The bimah can be a simple reading desk or an elaborate raised platform. It is usually placed in the middle of the sanctuary between the Holy Ark and the worshippers. The ceiling lamp, known as the Ner Tamid, Hebrew for "eternal lamp," symbolizes the Temple lamp that hung in front of the Ark. That Temple lamp consisted of a wick burning in oil, but today it is an electric light.

The Holy Ark can be a beautiful work of art.

Furnishings

The sanctuary comprises the largest area of the synagogue. Worshippers sit in wooden pews or on chairs facing the Holy Ark and the bimah. In an Orthodox synagogue, men and women sit apart, separated by a curtain or a screen called a *mekhitzah*. In some Orthodox synagogues, the women's section is in the balcony, and the men's section is on the main floor. Orthodox scholars say the practice is not intended to dishonor women but rather to prevent worshippers from being distracted while praying and communicating with God.

The sacred Torah scrolls are tied together with a sash and covered with an ornate velvet cloak embroidered with golden threads and ornamental beads. A silver crown, called the *keter*, is placed on the tops of both wooden shafts that extend above the scroll. A breastplate made of silver and etched with Jewish scriptures is attached to the Torah with a fine chain.

Because the Ten Commandments prohibit the making of carved images, statues and other forms of three-dimensional

A Torah scroll can be very large.

art are often avoided. Many sanctuaries have stained glass windows. Depictions of the Ten Commandments, the six-pointed Star of David, and menorahs—seven-branched candelabras—are decorations found in many synagogues.

The siddur is the main prayer book containing Jewish prayers. The chumash is a copy of the Torah in book form. In the United States, both books are often found in Hebrew with an English translation. In other countries, prayer books usually appear in Hebrew with a translation in the local language. Another prayer book, called the machzor, is used on Rosh Hashanah, which is the Jewish New Year, and on Yom Kippur.

Worship

Jewish religious services are held three times a day: in the morning, afternoon, and evening. Morning services are called shacharit, from the Hebrew word meaning "morning light." The afternoon prayer, minchah, takes its name from the ritual

MAKING A TORAH SCROLL

Creating a Torah scroll is a painstaking effort of labor and skill. A scribe trained in the laws regarding the proper writing and assembling of a scroll handwrites the scrolls. A scroll consists of between 62 and 84 sheets of varying sizes.[2] The sheets are specially prepared parchment made from animal skins. Each scroll contains exactly 304,805 letters, each carefully written in black ink with a feather quill.[3] After the writing is completed—which can take many months— the sheets of parchment are sewn together. Two wooden shafts are attached, one on each end of the scroll, around which the parchment is rolled. Torahs vary in size and weight, with the smallest weighing 5 pounds (2.3 kg) and the heaviest approximately 50 pounds (22.7 kg).[4]

Yarmulkes come in many colors and patterns.

offering of flour that accompanied sacrifices at the Temple in Jerusalem. Evening prayers—called maariv, from the Hebrew word meaning "bringing on night"—are recited after sunset.

Praying with a congregation is an essential element of Judaism. Some Jewish prayers and rituals require a minyan, a group of ten adults. Reform, Reconstructionist, and Conservative Judaism allow women to be included as part of the minyan, but Orthodox Judaism counts only adult males.

In Orthodox and Conservative synagogues, both men and women are required to wear head coverings during religious services. The male head covering is called a yarmulke or kippah. Women may wear scarves, hats, or chapel caps—small, flat lace kippahs. Traditionally, men wear a prayer shawl called a tallit during morning services and Yom Kippur services. Women in non-Orthodox congregations often wear tallitot (plural for tallit) as well. Reform Judaism does not insist on wearing either head coverings or tallitot.

Aside from Yom Kippur, the Sabbath is the holiest of all Jewish days. The Sabbath is a weekly event beginning at sunset on Friday evening and ending at sunset on Saturday. Each Sabbath morning, one portion of the Torah is read. Orthodox and some Conservative congregations read the entire Torah in one year. Reform and the remaining Conservative congregations read the Torah over a three-year period. At the start of the Torah service, the doors to the Holy Ark are opened. The entire congregation stands in respect for the sacredness of the Torah scrolls. One or more Torah scrolls may be removed at the same time, depending on the prayer service being held. Once the Torah is removed, the rabbi holds it aloft as the congregation chants the Shema. The scroll is carried around the room as the congregation sings. After the scroll makes its rounds, it is brought to the bimah. The ornaments and the velvet covering of the Torah are removed, and the scroll is rolled open upon the reading desk. Members of the congregation are usually invited up to the bimah to read from the Torah. Most synagogues call up several people to read during

THE CANTOR

In Judaism, a cantor is a trained vocalist who leads the congregation in singing the prayers. Also known as a hazan, meaning "overseer," professional cantors who have studied at cantorial schools are ordained clerics. In Reform, Reconstructionist, and Conservative Judaism, men or women may be cantors. In Orthodox Judaism, a cantor must be male. Cantors often serve as teachers and choir directors in Hebrew schools affiliated with the synagogue. All branches of Judaism allow non-clerics to lead the congregation in prayer.

SABBATH AT HOME

The Sabbath is a Jewish holy day, commanded by God to be a day of rest and religious observance. Sabbath rituals begin Friday evening with a member of the family setting the dinner table with two candles. The pair of candles represents God's commandment to both remember and observe the Sabbath. A glass of wine and two loaves of challah—a soft, sweet bread—are also placed on the table. Before sundown, the woman of the household lights the candles and recites a blessing.

Many families then attend evening services in the synagogue or perform them at home before eating dinner. After services, the parents bless their children, saying, "May God bless you and keep you. May God's presence radiate upon you and grant you graciousness. May God's presence be with you and grant you peace."[5]

Prior to enjoying the meal, a blessing called the kiddush is recited while holding the cup of wine. Each person then washes his or her hands while reciting a blessing. Finally, the head of the household says a prayer while holding the challah, thanking God, "who brings forth bread from the earth."[6] Pieces of the challah are passed around for everyone to eat. The family meal then begins.

the Sabbath services. At the conclusion of the Torah readings, special prayers are chanted for the ill, women who have just given birth, people who are soon to be married, and others.

The scroll is then lifted high for the entire congregation to see, and the decorations are placed back on the scroll. Before being returned to the Ark, the scroll is once again carried around the congregation. The scroll is returned to the Ark, the doors are closed, and the congregation sits down. The service then continues with additional prayers.

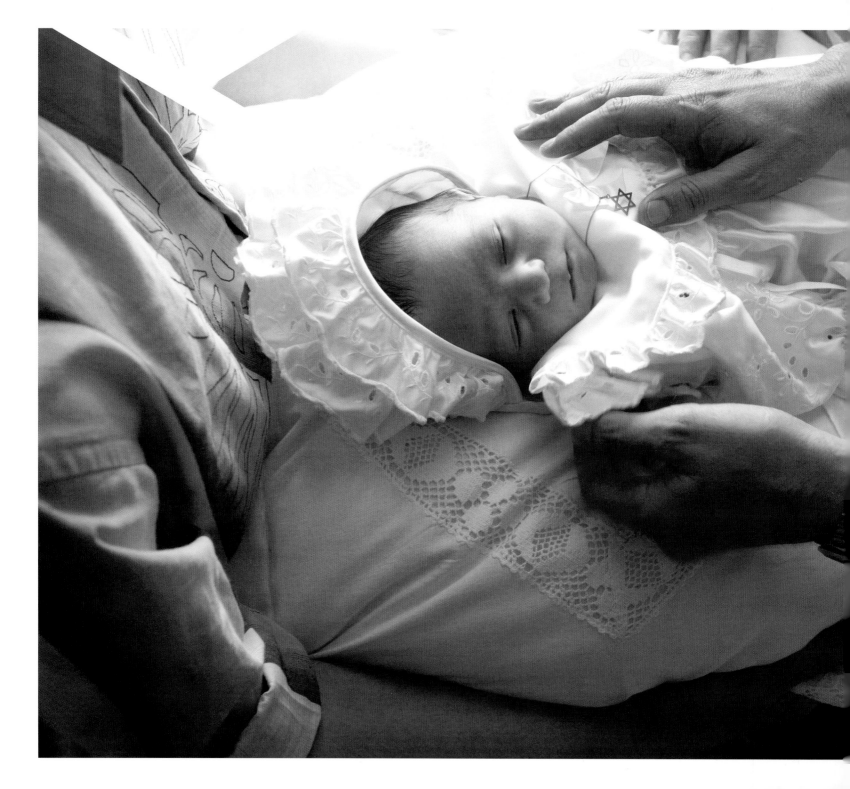

CHAPTER
EIGHT

RITUALS AND CELEBRATIONS

Jewish rituals, celebrations, and festivals are grounded in many centuries of Jewish history and law. According to Jewish law, life begins at birth, not at any earlier point during pregnancy or conception. Judaism teaches that a child is born free from sin. This is reflected in the daily prayer, "My God, the soul that You have given me is pure. You created it, You formed it, You breathed it into me."[1]

Though no laws dictate how Jewish parents must name their children, different traditions have developed, each designed to honor an ancestor of the newborn child. Among Ashkenazic Jews, the custom is to name the child after a family member, often a grandparent, who has recently died. Sephardic Jews traditionally name a new child after a living relative, also usually a grandparent. This practice allows grandparents to enjoy the honor of having a namesake while they are still alive.

Boys are named at a ceremony when they are eight days old. Girls are usually named within a week of birth.

Most Jewish children are given both a Hebrew name and a secular name. Today, it is common for Jewish parents to choose a Hebrew baby name that sounds similar to an English name. For example, a child may be given the Hebrew name Benzion ("Son of Zion") and be called Benson or Barry in English.

Baby boys are circumcised eight days after birth. God's commandment to circumcise appears in the Book of Genesis 17:10, as God makes his covenant with Abraham: "Such shall be the covenant between Me and you and your offspring to follow . . . every male among you shall be circumcised."[2] The circumcision is performed in the synagogue, the hospital, or in the parents' home. A mohel, a religious Jew who has been specially trained in surgical techniques, performs the procedure. Blessings and prayers are recited during the ceremony. Traditionally, the infant is named at the end of the ceremony.

Bar Mitzvah and Bat Mitzvah

In Jewish law, a boy is considered an adult at 13, and a girl is considered an adult at 12. At those ages, a boy has become a bar mitzvah ("son of the commandment") and a girl a bat mitzvah ("daughter of the commandment"). As adults in the Jewish community, both are now expected to obey halacha— Jewish law—and take on the responsibilities of adulthood. In Judaism, the young person may now lead religious services, be part of a minyan, and enter into legally binding contracts.

The bar mitzvah or bat mitzvah ceremony is usually conducted in the synagogue on the Sabbath as part of the morning religious services. It is marked by the young man's or young woman's first reading of the Torah. In some ceremonies, he or she may help lead part of the service or lead prayers. Addressing the congregation, the young person might explain a passage of the Bible or discuss an issue facing modern Judaism.

Marriage

Judaism views marriage as a sacred act, a divinely ordained union that fosters the continuation of the Jewish people. "It is not good for man to be alone," God says after creating Adam in the Book of Genesis 2:18.[3] The Talmud teaches that it is the duty of every Jewish father to ensure his son gets married.

In some synagogues, children might read the day's entire Torah portion for their bar mitzvahs or bat mitzvahs.

The marriage ceremony is conducted beneath the chuppah, which can be indoors or outdoors.

In Judaism, marriage is a legal agreement. Traditionally, the groom and the bride sign a contract called a ketubah. The practice of Jewish wedding contracts dates back to the time of the Talmud, and it is intended to protect the rights of married women. The ketubah document is often beautifully designed, incorporating ornate hand lettering and colorful art. Couples frequently frame the ketubah and display it in their home.

The ketubah obligates the groom to ensure his wife's financial needs are met and to provide food, medical care, clothing, and other necessities. Additionally, the husband agrees to provide for his wife after divorce. This provision is a protection for the wife because according to the Torah, only the husband can initiate a divorce. In modern times, Reform and Conservative Judaism recognize the rights of women to initiate divorce.

A Jewish wedding begins with the bride and groom standing beneath a chuppah, a type of canopy, with the parents standing alongside them. A rabbi conducts the marriage ceremony. A minyan is usually present for the ceremony. The groom places the wedding ring on his bride's finger, saying, "Be sanctified to me with this ring in accordance with the law of Moses and Israel."[4] By accepting the ring, the bride consents to be the groom's wife. Traditionally, the ceremony ends with a symbolic breaking of the wine glass from which the bride and groom sipped during the proceedings. The groom wraps the glass in a white cloth and places it on the ground. Then he steps on it with his right foot, smashing the glass. The breaking of the glass is said to commemorate the destruction of the First and Second Temples in Jerusalem. After the glass is broken, the guests erupt in joyous applause and congratulatory shouting.

Death

When a Jew dies, the body is covered in a plain white sheet. The corpse is not left alone until burial. It is instead guarded by a shomer, a watchman who remains with the body, reciting Psalms and other religious works to ease the deceased's soul. Before burial, the body is washed, wrapped in a white linen garment, and placed in a casket.

Jewish tradition calls for the body to be buried within 24 hours of death. The immediate family may be allowed to briefly view the body, but public viewings are prohibited. Burial may not be done on the Sabbath or on holy days. A religious service is held before burial, and a rabbi or family member presents a eulogy.

The casket is taken to the cemetery and placed in the ground. Each person attending the burial, starting with the family, puts shovelfuls of dirt into the grave until the casket is covered. Jews consider participation in burials a mitzvah, or good deed. When the burial is complete, the immediate family members recite the Mourner's Kaddish, a special prayer for the dead.

When the immediate family of the deceased returns home from the burial, they begin a period of mourning called shivah, which lasts seven days. During this time, the mourners sit on low boxes on the floor and are not permitted to go to work, shave, or study the Torah. Other family and friends visit the home to pay shivah calls consoling the mourners. At the home, a minyan gathers each morning and night to pray. Family mourners traditionally recite the Kaddish for the deceased daily for 11 months after the death. So the dead will not be forgotten, a tombstone is erected on the grave roughly one year following the burial. Inscribed on the tombstone is the deceased's name, usually in Hebrew, the dates of birth and death, and a Jewish symbol, such as a menorah, the Star of David, or the two tablets of the Ten Commandments.

Celebrations and Festivals: Rosh Hashanah

Jews also hold celebrations and festivals throughout the year. Rosh Hashanah, meaning the "head of the year," is the Jewish New Year. Rosh Hashanah falls on the first day of the Hebrew month Tishri,

The Jewish Calendar

Month	Order	Length in Days	Gregorian Calendar Equivalent
Nisan	1	30	March–April
Iyar	2	29	April–May
Sivan	3	30	May–June
Tammuz	4	29	June–July
Av	5	30	July–August
Elul	6	29	August–September
Tishri	7	30	September–October
Heshvan	8	29 or 30	October–November
Kislev	9	29 or 30	November–December
Tevet	10	29	December–January
Shevat	11	30	January–February
Adar/Adar II	12	29 (30 in leap year)/29 in leap year	February–March

Jewish holidays follow the Jewish calendar. This calendar does not have the same number of days as the Gregorian calendar used in the United States and many other countries. Approximately every three years, a second month of Adar is added to keep the Jewish calendar fairly in line with the Gregorian.

usually in September, and begins a ten-day period of repentance and seeking forgiveness, concluding with Yom Kippur. Rosh Hashanah begins in the evening with lighting candles and eating a family dinner at home, followed by services at the synagogue.

During the Rosh Hashanah morning service, the rabbi or another leader of the congregation blows the shofar. The piercing sound of the shofar symbolizes many important aspects of Judaism. It celebrates God as king, commemorates the giving of the Torah at Mount Sinai, and notifies people of the eventual coming of the Messiah at God's chosen time. In the afternoon, some congregations gather at a body of flowing water, such as the ocean, a stream, or a river. The worshippers toss stones or bread crumbs into the water, symbolically casting their sins to be washed away in the waters.

Yom Kippur

Yom Kippur, also called the Day of Atonement, falls on the tenth day of Tishri, ending the ten days of repentance that began with Rosh Hashanah. The holiest of all Jewish holidays, the Day of Atonement is a 25-hour day of intense praying, fasting, and seeking forgiveness from God. All Jewish adults are required to fast, though individuals may be excused if the fasting could adversely affect their health. The fast is said to be a punishment for sins during the previous year, and it helps the worshipper focus on prayer rather than food and drink.

The final service of Yom Kippur is called neilah (meaning "closing" or "locking"). Beginning as darkness falls on the second evening, neilah is the worshippers' final plea for God's forgiveness.

As the sun sets, praying becomes more intense and passionate. About one hour past sunset, the service draws to a dramatic close. The congregation fervently chants the Shema, repeating the words "The Lord is God" seven times. Then the shofar is blown, signaling the end of Yom Kippur. After services, family and friends return home to break the fast and enjoy a light meal.

Sukkoth

Sukkoth, a festival celebrating the fall harvest, begins on the fifteenth day of Tishri, less than one week after Yom Kippur. Traditionally, Jews build a temporary booth or hut called a sukkah, in which they live for seven days to remember the Exodus from Egypt and living in the desert wilderness en route to Israel. The roof of the sukkah is often made of leaves and branches. Fruits and vegetables are placed inside the sukkah, which is often adorned with decorations made by the children of the family.

During morning synagogue services, worshippers carry a palm branch and a lemonlike

SIMHATH TORAH

Simhath Torah is a one-day celebration that occurs at the end of Sukkoth. It is a joyous, festive occasion, a celebration of God's word. For one year, a different portion of the Torah has been read each Sabbath. On Simhath Torah, worshippers reach the end of the Torah and begin reading it all over once again.

Many congregations remove the Torah scrolls from the Holy Ark and carry them into the street, singing and dancing with the scrolls. Children happily join in the fun, receiving candy from the adults and parading around with tiny Torah scrolls of their own.

fruit called a citron while walking around the sanctuary and reciting hymns. The palm branch represents the strength of the Jewish people, and the citron represents the fruit of "the goodly tree" from the Bible.

Hanukkah

Hanukkah, meaning "dedication," celebrates the victory of the Maccabees over the Greeks in 164 BCE. This festive holiday, which usually falls in December, is also known as the Festival of Lights.

According to legend, the Maccabees recaptured the Temple in Jerusalem. They destroyed the Greek idols inside the Temple and purified the sanctuary, intending to restore the Temple back to the Jewish people. The religious ceremonies and celebration of rededicating the Temple were to take eight days. As the Maccabee leaders relit the sacred eternal lamp of the Temple, they discovered only one jar of purified oil, enough to last just one day. They lit the lamp, and the oil miraculously burned for eight days, enough time to make more oil.

In commemoration of the oil burning for eight days, Jewish families light Hanukkah candles on a menorah for eight nights. The Hanukkah menorah is a candelabra with nine branches. Every evening after sunset, candles are placed in the holders and lit while people say prayers thanking God for the miracle of Hanukkah. Among Judaism's most joyous celebrations, Hanukkah is a family time for parties, games, and gift giving.

Jews spend time with their families on Hanukkah.

Pesach

Pesach, or Passover, commemorates the Exodus of the ancient Hebrews from slavery in Egypt. The Exodus was a critical event in Jewish history, culminating in the establishment of the Jewish nation. The Seder, a ritual meal enjoyed on the first two nights of the eight-day holiday, is the main observance of Pesach. These festive occasions feature specially prepared foods, joyous songs, prayers of praise, and most importantly, the retelling of the Exodus from Egypt. Families gather around the dinner table and read from a book called the Haggadah ("telling"), which explains the events of the Jews' captivity in Egypt and their escape from bondage.

During the eight days of observance, Jews may not eat leavened bread. Instead, Jews eat matzah, a flat, dry, unleavened bread. Food made of leavened wheat, barley, rye, or oats—including pasta,

PURIM

The festival of Purim is between Hanukkah and Pesach. It commemorates the rescue of the Jewish people from death and annihilation in ancient Persia. The events that inspired the holiday appear in the Book of Esther. According to the account, Haman, an advisor to King Ahasuerus of Persia, condemns all Jews to be killed because a Jew named Mordecai refused to bow down to him. Neither the king nor Haman knows that Queen Esther is a Jew. Revealing her true religion, Esther tells Ahasuerus about Haman's plot and begs the king to save her people. Haman and his followers are put to death, and Mordecai is named an advisor to the king.

Purim is a favorite holiday of young children, who celebrate by wearing costumes, putting on plays, and making noise by banging on pots and pans or using groggers, a type of noisemaking toy. One of the main duties of the celebrants is to give to the poor and send gifts of food to friends as a means of giving thanks for being saved.

cereals, pizza, beer, and more—may not be eaten during Pesach. The matzah symbolizes the Hebrews' hasty escape from Egypt. With no time to wait for the yeast to make their dough rise, the slaves baked unleavened bread to take on their trek into the desert.

Shavuot

Shavuot is seven weeks after Pesach and commemorates the spring harvest and the giving of the Torah to Moses on Mount Sinai. The holiday is called for in Exodus 23:19 when the Hebrews are ordered, "The choice first fruits of your soil shall you bring to the house of the Lord your God."[5] In biblical times, the ancient Jews journeyed to Jerusalem from throughout the land to offer the first fruits and grains of their harvest at the Temple. God commanded the holiday as he entered into a

THE SEDER PLATE

The centerpiece of the dinner table at Pesach is the Seder plate. It traditionally contains six food items that symbolize the Pesach story:

1. A roasted or hard-boiled egg. The egg symbolizes the sacrifice offering on Jewish holidays at the Temple in Jerusalem. Also, the roundness of the egg represents the continuity of life.

2. Karpas, a green vegetable, usually parsley or celery. It represents springtime, the season during which Pesach occurs. During the Seder, the karpas is dipped in salt water or vinegar—symbolizing the tears shed by the enslaved Hebrews—and eaten.

3. A roasted lamb shank bone. This symbolizes the lamb sacrificed at the first Passover and at the Temple during Pesach.

4. Maror, or bitter herbs, usually horseradish. Maror is a modern-day reminder of the bitterness the Hebrew slaves endured in Egypt.

5. Haroseth, a sweet paste often made with chopped apples or dates, nuts, and wine. The thick mixture symbolizes the mortar used by the Hebrew slaves as they constructed buildings for the Egyptians.

6. Chazeret, a second bitter herb, often romaine lettuce. During the Seder, it is used to make matzah sandwiches with the maror.

Seder plates may also contain three pieces of matzah wrapped in a cloth. During the Seder meal, an adult hides the middle piece of matzah. After the Seder, the children are told to hunt for it. The lucky winner receives a small gift.

covenant with the Hebrews, giving the holiday a religious significance in addition to the importance of the crop harvest. The two-day festival centers on special prayers at the synagogue and studying the Torah into the late hours of the evening.

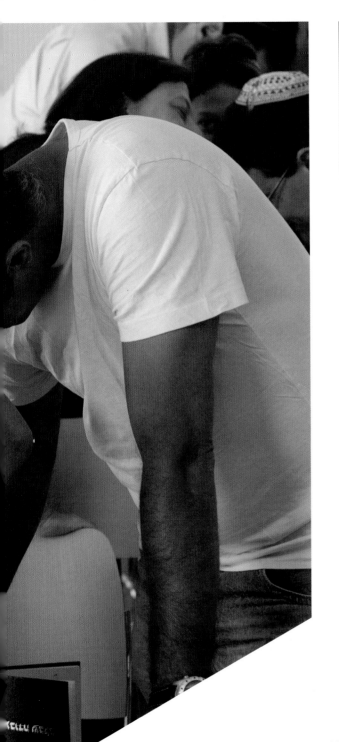
Judaism emphasizes the importance of family.

CHAPTER NINE

THE IMPACT OF JUDAISM

Three thousand years after Judaism first emerged in the Middle East, its impact on world civilization is still being felt to this day. Judaism crystallized the concept of monotheism and established the notion that the creator-God is omniscient, all powerful, and omnipresent. Judaism teaches that God created humans in his image and that, therefore, each life is sacred and special.

Life-Altering Concepts

In addition to shaping the notion of monotheism, Judaism also introduced the concept of a day of rest, the Sabbath. Today, the idea of resting for one day out of seven is nearly universally accepted. Acting morally and treating fellow humans fairly and equally are central teachings of Judaism. The Book of Leviticus 19:11 says, "You shall not deal deceitfully or falsely with one another."[1] Leviticus 19:15

GOOD AND EVIL

If God is good, how can there be so much evil and suffering in the world? If the Jews are truly God's "chosen people," how could God permit the Holocaust to happen? For millennia, Jews have struggled to explain the problem of evil.

Rabbis and biblical scholars differ widely on the issue. The biblical explanation begins with God's granting humans free will—the freedom to do good or evil. When people choose to be good, God rewards them. When they do evil, God punishes them. Evil, therefore, is the result of humans making sinful choices. God is not responsible for evil.

But why do bad things happen to good people? Regarding the Jews, some scholars believe the Jewish people are God's "suffering servant," mentioned in the Book of Isaiah. One rabbi argues evil exists because God has limited power. He does not control the universe, and therefore bad things happen. The horrors of the Holocaust prompted many Jews to believe that there is no God, or that he simply doesn't care about humankind. Overall, Judaism's explanations for evil are as diverse as its attitudes toward many other areas in life.

says, "Do not favor the poor or show deference to the rich; judge your kinsman fairly."[2] The Torah insists all people are equal under the law.

Under Moses, the Israelites established one of the world's first comprehensive systems of courts, from local courts dealing with minor disputes to high courts ruling on the most important cases. Today, most of the world's nations use a similar legal system. The Bible establishes rules about agricultural techniques, many still used on modern farms. Crop rotation was introduced in the Book of Exodus: "Six years you shall sow your land and gather in its yield, but in the seventh year you shall let it rest and lie fallow."[3]

Science, Medicine, Philosophy, and More

Though Jews are few in number compared to members of other major world religions, Jewish contributions to society are great in both quantity and quality. In medicine, it was a Jew who developed the first polio vaccine (Jonas Salk), conducted research that led to the discovery of insulin (Moses Barron), pioneered anticancer chemotherapy (Isadore Ravdin), discovered the antibiotic streptomycin (Selman Waksman), and performed the first successful bone marrow transplant (William Dameshek), among others. Notable Jewish scientists include Albert Einstein, Niels Bohr, and Richard Feynman. Jewish thinkers who have made important contributions in their fields include psychologists Sigmund Freud, Alfred Adler, Abraham Maslow, Leon Festinger, and Holocaust survivor Viktor Frankl. Many Jewish philosophers' works have drawn worldwide attention as well.

FAMOUS JEWISH ATHLETES

Jews have a long and successful history in the world of sports. Swimmer Mark Spitz won 11 medals at Summer Olympics games, including 7 gold medals.[4] Gymnast Agnes Keleti won a total of 10 Olympic medals, including 5 golds, at the 1952 and 1956 games.[5] Boxer Barney Ross was a world champion in 3 weight divisions during the 1930s.[6] In recent years, basketball player Sue Bird has won 2 Women's National Basketball Association championships and 4 Olympic gold medals.[7] Outstanding baseball players Sandy Koufax and Hank Greenberg are members of the National Baseball Hall of Fame.

Jewish Nobel Prize winners in literature and fiction include Bob Dylan and Nadine Gordimer. Edna Ferber, Art Spiegelman, Norman Mailer, Geraldine Brooks, Louis Simpson, Anthony Hecht, and Maxine Kumin are among Jewish Pulitzer Prize winners. Great Jewish music composers include Felix Mendelssohn, Gustav Mahler, George Gershwin, and Aaron Copland, while Jascha Heifetz, Isaac Stern, and Itzhak Perlman are among the world's finest violinists.

Judaism teaches the practice of *tikkun olam*, meaning "world repair." In modern Jewish life, tikkun olam is achieved through human actions in the pursuit of social justice. It is each Jew's responsibility to help improve the world for himself or herself and for the betterment of future generations. Dozens of Jewish-managed foundations in the United States support Jewish and general causes, such as education, the arts, at-risk youth, and the preservation of green space.

The Future

Among the greatest challenges facing Judaism today is the increasing assimilation of the Jewish people. In some cases, this has continued to cause tensions. A resurgence of anti-Semitism in Western Europe, the Muslim world, and the United States is another troubling concern for Jews and Judaism. In France, Jews have been attacked and Jewish schools burned. In Turkey, suicide bombers have attacked synagogues while worshippers attended Sabbath services. A report released by the Pew Research Center in 2017 details other recent incidents of anti-Semitism that have occurred across Russia, Italy, the United Kingdom, Ukraine, and many other countries. In April 2017, a study released by the Anti-Defamation League revealed that anti-Semitic incidents in the United States grew by more than one-third from 2015 to 2016 and skyrocketed by more than 85 percent from 2016 to the first three months of 2017.[8]

Assimilation also presents another issue. Many Jews believe Judaism is in danger of disappearing through assimilation and marriage to non-Jews. They fear such intermarriage results in the weakening of Jewish values and culture, and at worst, the possible abandonment of Judaism altogether. The results of a poll conducted by the Pew Research Center in 2013 showed that increasing numbers of Jews are not religious. In addition, during the years 2005 to 2013, 58 percent of Jews married a non-Jewish spouse—up from 17 percent

PERSPECTIVES

CECIL ROTH

Jewish historian Cecil Roth was born in London, England, in 1899. A religious Jew, he studied at Merton College in Oxford, earning his PhD in 1924. When the Nazis began persecuting the Jews of Germany in the early 1930s, Roth strongly protested the oppression in a series of articles and books. In all, he wrote more than 600 books and articles in his lifetime, including histories about Sephardic Jews, Chinese Jews, and the Jews of England.[9] One of Roth's most popular works is *A History of the Jews*, published in 1961. He writes:

> *Today, the Jewish people has in it still those elements of strength and endurance which enabled it to surmount all the crises of its past, surviving thus the most powerful empires of antiquity.*
>
> *Throughout our history there have been weaker elements who have shirked the sacrifices which Judaism entailed. They have been swallowed, long since, in the great majority; only the more stalwart have carried on the traditions of their ancestors, and can now look back with pride upon their superb heritage. Are we to be numbered with the weak majority, or with the stalwart minority? It is for ourselves to decide.[10]*

Roth died in 1970 at the age of 71 in Jerusalem.

An activist wears a star similar to those the Nazis made Jews wear. The words "never again" show the protestor's disapproval of anti-Semitism.

before 1970—and many Jews are raising their children outside the Jewish faith.[11] Some Jews, however, believe increased assimilation has benefits for the Jewish community. Rabbi Michael Knopf of Virginia believes that Jews can work with and learn from non-Jews to strengthen Judaism.

Modern Jews are tackling ethical and moral challenges, such as the issues of homosexuality, birth control, and abortion. Each branch of Judaism views these matters differently, underscoring yet another challenge to future generations of Jews: the tensions between the Reform, Conservative, Orthodox, and Reconstructionist movements.

Judaism's survival in the face of persecution and oppression is an exceptional, uplifting story. Thousands of years after the emergence of Judaism, Jewish religion, values, and traditions remain vibrant and inspiring. Predicting the future of Judaism is a difficult task, but history teaches that the Jewish people have always adapted to changing times, and that shows no signs of stopping now.

ESSENTIAL FACTS

DATE FOUNDED

Judaism was founded roughly 3,000 years ago in the Middle East.

BASIC BELIEFS

Judaism is based on monotheism, the belief in a single creator-God. The God of the Jewish people is omniscient, all powerful, and omnipresent—though not in everything. Traditionally, Jews believe God is separate and above his creation—humanity and the universe—but is involved in the natural and human events on Earth. The Hebrew Bible or Tanakh contains the Torah, the holy scripture of Judaism, given by God to Moses on Mount Sinai.

IMPORTANT HOLIDAYS AND EVENTS

- ⊙ Rosh Hashanah, the Jewish New Year

- ⊙ Yom Kippur, the Day of Atonement

- ⊙ Sukkoth, a harvest festival

- ⊙ Hanukkah, the Festival of Lights

- ⊙ Purim, which commemorates the rescue of the Jewish people from death and annihilation in ancient Persia

- ⊙ Pesach, or Passover, which celebrates the Exodus of the Hebrews from Egyptian slavery

- ⊙ Shavuot, which commemorates the spring harvest and the giving of the Torah to Moses on Mount Sinai

FAITH LEADERS

- Abraham was the first of the Hebrew patriarchs who obeyed the commands of God, with whom he made the sacred covenant.

- Moses led the Hebrews out of slavery in Egypt and received the Torah with the Ten Commandments from God on Mount Sinai.

- Rabbi Moses Maimonides was a Sephardic Jewish philosopher of the 1100s CE. He is best remembered for his writings on religion, notably the Thirteen Principles of Faith.

NUMBER OF PEOPLE WHO PRACTICE JUDAISM

The Jewish world population is roughly 14 million people.

QUOTE

"Throughout our history there have been weaker elements who have shirked the sacrifices which Judaism entailed. They have been swallowed, long since, in the great majority; only the more stalwart have carried on the traditions of their ancestors, and can now look back with pride upon their superb heritage. Are we to be numbered with the weak majority, or with the stalwart minority? It is for ourselves to decide."

—*Cecil Roth*, History of the Jews *(1961)*

GLOSSARY

ASSIMILATION
The process of adopting the ways of another culture.

ATONEMENT
A theological concept that describes how humans ask God to forgive them.

AUTHORITATIVE
Accurate and reliable.

CANTOR
The official who leads the congregation in the musical portion of a Jewish religious service.

CHARACTER
A person's collection of values and moral traits.

CONVERT
To adopt a new religion as one's own.

COVENANT
A formal, binding agreement.

LGBTQ
An acronym used to describe nonheterosexual people: lesbian, gay, bisexual, transgender, and queer or questioning.

OMNIPRESENT
The state of being everywhere at all times.

OMNISCIENT
All knowing.

ORDAIN
To appoint as a rabbi, minister, or priest. Also, to establish.

PATRIARCH
The father or male leader of a family or clan.

PHILOSOPHY

The attempt to gain wisdom through thinking.

PLAGUE

A disease or other physical evil that afflicts a group.

PROPHECY

A message from a divine figure, sometimes including predictions of the future.

RABBI

A teacher trained in Jewish law and ordained for leadership of a Jewish congregation.

RIGHTEOUS

Someone who is without sin and behaves according to divine law.

SACRED

Something that is set apart for religious purposes and should be treated with respect.

SANCTUARY

The most important room of a synagogue, where the Holy Ark is kept and services are held.

SECULAR

Nonreligious.

SHOFAR

A trumpet made of a ram, goat, gazelle, or antelope horn, sounded during Rosh Hashanah and at the end of Yom Kippur.

YEAST

A baking ingredient that causes dough and batter to rise.

ADDITIONAL RESOURCES

SELECTED BIBLIOGRAPHY

Baskin, Judith R., and Kenneth Seeskin, eds. *The Cambridge Guide to Jewish History, Religion, and Culture*. New York: Cambridge UP, 2010. Print.

Karesh, Sara E., and Mitchell M. Hurvitz. *Encyclopedia of Judaism*. New York: Facts on File, 2006. Print.

Maher, Michael. *Judaism: An Introduction to the Beliefs and Practices of the Jews*. Dublin, Ireland: Columbia Press, 2006. Print.

Robinson, George. *Essential Judaism: A Complete Guide to Beliefs, Customs, and Rituals*. New York: Pocket Books, 2000. Print.

Stefon, Matt, ed. *Judaism: History, Belief, and Practice*. New York: Britannica Educational Publishing, 2012. Print.

FURTHER READINGS

Lusted, Marcia Amidon. *The Israeli-Palestinian Conflict*. Minneapolis: Abdo, 2018. Print.

Owings, Lisa. *Israel*. Minneapolis: Abdo, 2013. Print.

Perl, Lila, and Marion Blumenthal Lazan. *Four Perfect Pebbles: A True Story of the Holocaust*. New York: Greenwillow, 2016. Print.

ONLINE RESOURCES

To learn more about Judaism, visit **abdobooklinks.com**. These links are routinely monitored and updated to provide the most current information available.

MORE INFORMATION

For more information on this subject, contact or visit the following organizations:

JEWISH MUSEUM

1109 Fifth Avenue
New York, NY 10128
212-423-3200
thejewishmuseum.org

Exhibits at the Jewish Museum reveal thousands of years of Jewish culture from around the world.

US HOLOCAUST MEMORIAL MUSEUM

100 Raoul Wallenberg Place SW
Washington, DC 20024-2126
202-488-0400
ushmm.org

The United States' official memorial to the Holocaust offers exhibits, film footage, and personal stories to document the Holocaust.

SOURCE NOTES

Chapter 1. An Ancient Religion

1. "The Shema." *My Jewish Learning.* My Jewish Learning, 2018. Web. 31 Jan. 2018.

2. "The Shema."

3. "Vital Statistics: Jewish Population of the World." *Jewish Virtual Library.* American-Israeli Cooperative Enterprise, 2018. Web. 31 Jan. 2018.

4. "Vital Statistics."

Chapter 2. Origins and Foundations

1. Leonard Woolley. "Ur." *Encyclopaedia Britannica.* Encyclopaedia Britannica, 2018. Web. 31 Jan. 2018.

2. "Psalm 23." *Bible Gateway.* Bible Gateway, n.d. Web. 31 Jan. 2018.

3. Tabor, James. "Masada: Cave 2000/2001." *The Jewish Roman World of Jesus.* UNC Charlotte, n.d. Web. 31 Jan. 2018.

Chapter 3. Into the Modern Era

1. "The Holocaust: An Introductory History." *Jewish Virtual Library.* American-Israeli Cooperative Enterprise, 2018. Web. 31 Jan. 2018.

2. Pierre Van Paassen. *The Forgotten Ally.* New York: Dial, 1943. Print. 45.

3. "Documenting the Number of Victims of the Holocaust and Nazi Persecution." *Holocaust Encyclopedia.* United States Holocaust Memorial Museum, n.d. Web. 31 Jan. 2018.

4. "The Killing Machine: The Concentration Camps, 1933–1945." *Holocaust: A Call to Conscience.* Projetaladin.org, 2009. Web. 31 Jan. 2018.

Chapter 4. What Jews Believe

1. Wayne Dosick. *Living Judaism: The Complete Guide to Jewish Belief, Tradition and Practice*. San Francisco: HarperSanFrancisco, 1995. Print. 19.

2. Adele Berlin and Marc Zvi Brettler, eds. *The Jewish Study Bible*. New York: Oxford UP, 2004. Print. 1181.

3. "What Do Jews Believe About Jesus?" *My Jewish Learning*. My Jewish Learning, 2018. Web. 31 Jan. 2018.

4. Simcha Paull Raphael. *Jewish Views of the Afterlife*. Northvale, NJ: J. Aronson, 1994. Print. 304.

Chapter 5. Sacred Scriptures

1. Adele Berlin and Marc Zvi Brettler, eds. *The Jewish Study Bible*. New York: Oxford UP, 2004. Print. 14.

2. Stephen H. Arnoff. "Seder Nashim (Women)." *My Jewish Learning*. My Jewish Learning, 2018. Web. 31 Jan. 2018.

3. Mendy Hecht. "The 613 Commandments." *Chabad.org*. Chabad-Lubavitch Media Center, 2018. Web. 31 Jan. 2018.

Chapter 6. Different Voices: The Branches of Judaism

1. Laurie Goodstein. "Poll Shows Major Shift in Identity of US Jews." *New York Times*. New York Times, 1 Oct. 2013. Web. 31 Jan. 2018.

2. "Reconstructionism." *Reconstructing Judaism*. Reconstructing Judaism, n.d. Web. 31 Jan. 2018.

SOURCE NOTES CONTINUED

Chapter 7. The Synagogue

1. "Tehillim—Psalms—Chapter 23." *Chabad.org*. Chabad-Lubavitch Media Center, 2018. Web. 31 Jan. 2018.

2. "Basic Laws Regarding Torah Scrolls." *Keddem Congregation*. Keddem, n.d. PDF. 31 Jan. 2018.

3. "In Pictures: Writing a Torah Scroll." *BBC News*. BBC, 27 July 2013. Web. 31 Jan. 2018.

4. "Torah Is Heavy, Man." *Ohr Somayach*. Ohr Somayach International, n.d. Web. 31 Jan. 2018.

5. "Shabbat: Shabbat Evening Home Rituals." *Jewish Virtual Library*. American-Israeli Cooperative Enterprise, 2018. Web. 31 Jan. 2018.

6. "Shabbat Evening Home Rituals."

Chapter 8. Rituals and Celebrations

1. "Elohai N'shama—My Pure Soul." *Beth Sholom B'nai Israel*. Beth Sholom B'nai Israel, 2018. Web. 31 Jan. 2018.

2. Adele Berlin and Marc Zvi Brettler, eds. *The Jewish Study Bible*. New York: Oxford UP, 2004. Print. 38.

3. Berlin and Brettler, 16.

4. "Under the Huppah: The Jewish Wedding." *The Pluralism Project: America's Many Religions*. President and Fellows of Harvard College and Diana Eck, 2018. Web. 31 Jan. 2018.

5. Berlin and Brettler, 160.

Chapter 9. The Impact of Judaism

1. Adele Berlin and Marc Zvi Brettler, eds. *The Jewish Study Bible*. New York: Oxford UP, 2004. Print. 253.

2. Berlin and Brettler, 254.

3. Berlin and Brettler, 158.

4. "Mark Sptiz." *SR/Olympic Sports*. Sports Reference, 2016. Web. 31 Jan. 2018.

5. "Ãgnes Keleti." *SR/Olympic Sports*. Sports Reference, 2016. Web. 31 Jan. 2018.

6. Neil Francis Milbert. "Barney Ross." *Encyclopaedia Britannica*. Encyclopaedia Britannica, 2018. Web. 31 Jan. 2018.

7. "About Sue Bird." *WNBA*. NBA Media Ventures, 2018. Web. 31 Jan. 2018.

8. "US Anti-Semitic Incidents Spike 86 Percent So Far in 2017 after Surging Last Year, ADL Finds." *ADL*. Anti-Defamation League, 2017. Web. 31 Jan. 2018.

9. "Cecil Roth." *Oxford Chabad Society— Serving Oxford Jewish Students*. Chabad.org, 2018. Web. 31 Jan. 2018.

10. Cecil Roth. *A History of the Jews*. New York: Schocken, 1961. Print. 423.

11. "A Portrait of Jewish Americans." *Religion & Public Life*. Pew Research Center, 1 Oct. 2013. Web. 31 Jan. 2018.

INDEX

ABOUT THE AUTHOR

Nel Yomtov is an award-winning author of nonfiction books and graphic novels for young readers. His writing passions include history, geography, military, nature, sports, biographies, and careers. Yomtov has also written, edited, and colored hundreds of Marvel comic books. Yomtov has served as editorial director of a children's nonfiction book publisher and as executive editor of Hammond World Atlas book division. Yomtov lives in the New York City area with his wife.

Yomtov would like to dedicate this book to the memory of the Jewish residents of Janina, Greece, who were victims of the Holocaust.